RENEWING YOUR
Mind

A Guide To Transforming Your World
From Chaos To Clarity

By Makini Smith & Suzana Mihajlovic

The events and conversations in this book have been set down to the best of the author's ability.

The publishers will be pleased to make good any omissions or rectify any mistakes brought to their attention at the earliest opportunity. Any internet addresses, phone numbers, or company or product information printed in this book are offered as a resource and are not intended in any way to be or to imply an endorsement by the author/publisher, nor does they vouch for the existence, content, or services of these sites, phone numbers, companies, or products beyond the life of this book.

First paperback edition September 2022

Book design Kamar Martin

ISBN 978-1-9990240-4-8 (Paperback)
ISBN 978-1-9990240-5-5 (Hardcover)
ISBN 978-1-9990240-6-2 (Ebook)

www.awalkinmystilettos.com

www.your2minds.com

"Do not be conformed to this world but be transformed by the renewal of your mind, that by testing you may discern what is the will of God, what is good and acceptable and perfect."

Romans 12:2 (English Standard Version)

Table of contents

Prayer vii

Dedication ix

Foreword: By Brian Proctor; Son of Bob Proctor xi

Renewing Your Mind: Introduction 1

Chapter 1: Honoring Your Present Moment 5

Chapter 2: Self Care for the Mind, Body, and Soul 13

Chapter 3: Your Deeper Purpose 31

Chapter 4: Overcoming Your Fears 53

Chapter 5: Goal Setting 75

Chapter 6: Habits 99

Chapter 7: How deep is your desire 119

Moving Forward 127

About The Authors: Suzana Mihajlovic 131

About The Authors: Makini Smith 135

Prayer

Dear Lord,

Thank you for bringing us together in the creation of this book. Thank you for bringing us together with our readers. We ask that you look over us all, guide us, and guide our readers to their highest potential. We ask that you give us strength, character and a vision that comes from deep within our soul. Thank you for your guidance in realizing our vision. That is your gift to each of us. Inspire us, guide us and pull us to what is yours, what is ours, what is good. Help us all understand a more profound mission and purpose in this life and why we are here in the physical body. Fill our hearts with the joy of your truth and the awe of being alive. Let the renewing of our minds transform us.

Thank you, Father. In your name, it is so.

Dedication

This book is dedicated to our mentor and dear friend Bob Proctor. Bob has been our most outstanding teacher and mentor. We are grateful to have had the opportunity to work with one of the greatest legends in human potential that walked this planet. Our purpose is to continue to help change the world one person at a time through Bob's legacy and teachings. Thank you, dear Bob, for all that you have taught us, for stretching us to our more significant potential and for being the most incredible mentor of all time. Thank you for your impeccable belief in us and for investing your time to help us experience more of what we are capable of and tap into our fullest potential. We will carry your belief in us, deliver your vision, and continue improving our work daily. We love you, dear Bob.

In loving memory of Bob Proctor 1934-2022

REST IN PEACE

Foreword

There are not a lot of people that I know who are truly living the way they want to live. Most people are just going daily without a real sense of purpose. Do you have a dream, or have you given up on that dream? It could just be a matter of feeling stuck.

Let's face it; we are living in interesting times. I firmly believe that now more than ever, we need to be careful of our thoughts. I like how Suzana and Makini discuss the power of meditation and how it can change our outlook on everything around us and, in turn, our thoughts for the better.

This book, Renewing Your Mind, has some critical components to getting clear on your purpose. Within these pages are tools to help you get clear on your dream again and then how to move forward to living that life you have always wanted.

I have had the great pleasure of knowing Suzana Mihajlovic for several years now. I have personally seen how she has changed her life for the better, both personally and in her business. Suzana and Makini have clearly documented the strategies that they have used to change not only their lives but the lives of their clients.

My father, Bob Proctor, instilled in me all of my life how the power of gratitude can completely change the course of your day. As you read this book, you will see how and why to use gratitude. I know this book will change the way you have thought of gratitude in the past. True freedom comes from within. Let Makini and Suzana guide you so that you take control of your life from within; it is all here.

You have picked up this book for a reason. Are you ready to get past the things that block you? If so, keep reading. Dig in and really enjoy.

Brian Proctor

Renewing Your Mind: Introduction

There is no denying that the world is currently going through a very challenging time. In the quest for our daily purpose and work, we have been experiencing a shift. To serve individuals to break through to their higher purpose, their dream. There has been a general feeling of fear, heaviness, anxiety, and uncertainty amongst most people living today. It seems to be a collective *"dark night of the soul,"* a thickness that most people speak of feeling.

This experience is something that maybe many coaches would say, *"Don't think about it. Think only of the positive."* Our stance is slightly different from theirs, so we have written this book. It can be called your companion during these interesting times. We are not afraid to delve into these genuine and natural emotions. We understand that the depth of our challenges is also the depth of our awakening. The human race is currently in the discomfort of the cocoon, both individually and collectively. Yet it is a necessary stage of the complete process of the metamorphosis - the transformation from which we will experience a new dawn with much greater certainty, an awakening that will bring a real depth of beauty, wisdom, and an innate understanding that we are not alone. We rely on each other. A wealth of potential lies within us that needs a dark night to awaken the new dawn of this potential's true and exquisite power.

The Bible verse from Romans 12:2 (English Standard Version) is a perfect reminder of the times we are living in:

"Do not be conformed to this world but be transformed by the renewal of your mind, that by testing you may discern what is the will of God, what is good and acceptable and perfect."

We live in times where fear bombards us every day. It is all around us, and we have been deceived with messages to be afraid of each other. We have been confined to our homes, sometimes for months, depending on what part of the world we dwell in. Times have changed so swiftly.

How does a once "free person" stay free in such restrictive and fearful times? Our perspective is not political but aims to show you that true freedom always comes from within. Therefore, no matter the message we receive from external forces, we can remain free to stick with some daily disciplines to help us thrive and get through these challenging times.

We must renew our minds to stay in the truth of who we are. Otherwise, we become a servant to the world outside of us. We repeat the Biblical quote in Romans 12:2:

"Do not be conformed to this world but be transformed by the renewal of your minds..."

As demanding life in the 2020s may be feeling for most right now, we always have a choice. We can conform to the fear, the world, and the messages or transform our lives by renewing our minds. So, you see, you can feel the discomfort and choose to move through it into growth and power. The development and true power come from choosing to discipline your mindset to keep you with the truth — your truth. Your authentic power will be within your vision and soul rather than consumed and controlled by fear and hopelessness.

And *"that by testing you may discern what is the will of God, what is good and acceptable and perfect."*

By staying aware of the messages surrounding you and externally, you can consciously assess whether the world's ideas are a truth you would like to adopt for yourself. You also have the choice to reject these messages and stay with the truth of God. The fact is that you are perfect, whole and complete. You have more power within than you can ever imagine. The truth is that you have everything inside you to create a new reality, new freedom. We cannot buy this freedom; it can only be experienced. And this can be accomplished by renewing your mind and accepting good, acceptable *and perfect* thoughts.

So, this book is a gift to you. As we have mentioned, it is a companion. It gives you basic steps and reminders that you can implement immediately to renew your mind, body and soul.

Chapter 1:

~

Honoring Your Present Moment

"Yesterday is history. Tomorrow is a mystery. Today is a gift. That is why it is called the present."
— Alice Morse Earle.

W e ask you to open your mind to the ideas we will share. And let's have some fun.

We're going to be starting with the current situation. We need to acknowledge where we are now to move forward and change anything. It is essential to honor your present surroundings. So, we ask that you take a second to open up your mind because a closed mind cannot accept new ideas. We want to make sure that you can receive everything we have to share with you.

My first question for you is, where are you now?

What are you feeling today?

How is your heart?

What is your present state of mind?

Let's go further into honoring this moment.

There's so much chaos happening. People feel stressed, overwhelmed and anxious, and it's become our new normal. Our brains are not designed to deal with so much uncertainty for such a long period.

We're not giving ourselves grace, and we're hard on ourselves. With everything that is happening, it's hard to have the capacity to function like we usually do. So many of us feel like we're performing slower or not at a pace that we're used to.

There is a term for how you are feeling. It's called *languishing*.

Languishing describes a mental state that may make it hard for you to feel optimistic about your life. People who feel this way lack the same joy they once had. They may feel a general deficiency of mental well-being, but they do not have depression or other diagnosed mental health conditions.

When you're in this mental state, you may not see the point of things. It's hard to look forward to new or positive directions in your life. You're not necessarily feeling hopeless. You're languishing.

The term languishing originates with international researchers, including sociologist Dr. Corey Keyes, who defines it as a previously overlooked clinical state.

Symptoms may be unique to each person but include:

- A sense of feeling stuck, or that life has become stagnant

- Feelings of emptiness

- Lack of motivation

- A sense of mental malaise (general lack of well-being)

While languishing is not a formal mental health diagnosis, the emotions are valid and authentic. In positive psychology, which centers on experiences and circumstances that contribute to well-being, flourishing is considered the state in which a person feels positive emotions toward life in general. This allows them to function mentally, emotionally, and socially. In other words, flourishing refers to mental wellness.

On the other hand, the concept of languishing focuses on the absence of such mental wellness. You don't have positive emotions toward life, leading you to experience mental, emotional, and relational challenges. But languishing is not the same as depression, even though it's also associated with emotional distress. Instead, it's a middle point in the mental health continuum that ranges from mental health and wellness to mental health conditions.

Some experts associate languishing with overall feelings of emptiness or just not feeling anything at all. In other words, you may feel different — low — but not experience any extreme negative emotions. With languishing, you may not experience significant symptoms of depression, but you're not functioning well socially or psychologically either.

We want you to give yourself some grace. What we focus on grows. What we give our attention to consumes us. When our feelings consume us, it fills the mind and crowds all other ideas out of consciousness. However, we don't believe in contributing to toxic positivity.

Toxic positivity is the excessive and ineffective overgeneralization of a happy, optimistic state for all situations. The process of harmful positivity results in the denial, minimization and invalidation of the authentic human emotional experience. Like anything done in excess, using positivity to cover up or silence the human experience becomes toxic. By disallowing the existence of certain feelings, we fall into a state of denial and repressed emotions.

We don't believe in contributing to toxic positivity because it can harm people going through difficult times. People find their feelings dismissed, ignored, or outright invalidated rather than sharing genuine human emotions and gaining unconditional support.

- **It's shaming:** When someone is suffering, they need to know that their emotions are valid, but they can find support and love in their friends and family. Toxic positivity tells people that the feelings they are experiencing are unacceptable.

- **It causes guilt:** It sends a message that if you aren't finding a way to feel positive, you are doing something wrong even in the face of adversity.

- **It avoids authentic human emotion:** Toxic positivity functions as an avoidance mechanism. When we feel complex emotions, we discount, dismiss and deny them. When other people engage in this type of behavior, it can sidestep emotional situations that may make them feel uncomfortable.

- **It prevents growth:** It allows us to avoid feeling things that might be painful, but it also denies us the ability to face challenging feelings that can ultimately lead to growth and deeper insight.

It is possible to be optimistic in the face of difficult experiences and challenges. But people going through traumatic experiences don't need to be told to stay positive or feel that we will judge them for not maintaining a "good vibes only" attitude.

So, we're not going to suggest only focusing on the light. But we do have to acknowledge the dark, the shadow, the things we may not necessarily want to deal with to move on, evolve and move forward.

So let's take a second. Where are you presently?

What are you feeling? Your feelings are valid. Our feelings are data. Just as how we think needs to be assessed, so do our feelings. What are we doing with that information if we don't recognize our own emotions or others'?

Feelings are data. Yes, feelings change, but we need to pay attention to how we feel. There are underlying reasons for our feelings and what triggers them. Are those feelings being assessed?

1. We need to recognize our own emotions and those of others. What is the source?

2. Label our emotions. Those labels explain the vibration we are on. For example, sad = low vibration. Excited = high vibration.

3. Regulate our emotions rather than let them regulate us. We have the power to control ourselves.

We need to understand how we're feeling to connect with other people and know how they feel to have some empathy and compassion. So look at your present state. Pay attention to what you're feeling. What is the source of that? Where are those feelings coming from?

When dealing with these emotions, those feelings are not permanent. So please think about that. We may presently be in a state, but note that it is not permanent.

What is the information telling you? What do you need to change?

We invite you to acknowledge where you are. Label your feelings, don't suppress them. We recognize them to express them because unexpressed feelings can pile up like bad debt. You don't want to do that.

We have all these feelings that we're not acknowledging or expressing. We suppress them. And when we start to silence our emotions, it causes issues like depression, anger, outbursts, and all types of negative behavior because we've tucked them deep down. We need to be able to process these feelings.

Processing and allowing feelings to run through us may be challenging, especially when feeling overwhelmed. Remind yourself that your feelings are energy and will enable the energy to pass through your body. Let's explore some self-care techniques to help you get through emotionally challenging times.

Chapter 2:

~

Self Care for the Mind, Body, and Soul

"If you don't love yourself, nobody will. Not only that, you won't be good at loving anyone else. Loving starts with the self." – Wayne Dyer

It is essential to take care of all three aspects of your being - your mind, your body and your soul.

When your emotions are challenging to process, the following self-care techniques can help you. We'll give you three things for each section to help you get through these uncertain times.

MIND

- Read 20 minutes or ten pages per day.

- Listen to soothing music that makes you feel good.

- Spend time alone to eliminate outside distractions.

BODY

- Sip on a gallon of water throughout the day.

- Get seven to eight hours of sleep at night.

- Stay physically active.

SOUL

- Prayer and meditation.

- Gratitude and affirmations.

- A community of healthy connections.

Self-care for the mind

Daily reading has so many benefits. It helps with keeping our minds renewed. Whether it's an article or a book, exercise our brains by reading every day. Whatever it is, we try to ensure that we're reading something daily.

Try to commit to twenty minutes a day minimum or ten pages out of a book per day to ensure that you consistently keep up with educating yourself and keeping your mind sharp.

When was the last time you read a book or a substantial magazine article?

Reading has a significant number of benefits, including, but not limited to:

- Mental stimulation
- Knowledge
- Stress reduction
- Vocabulary expansion
- Memory improvement
- Stronger analytical thinking skills
- Improved focus and concentration
- Better writing skills
- Tranquility
- Entertainment

Step away from your computer and put down your phone for a little while. Crack open a book, and replenish your mind.

The second self-care tool to calm your mind is listening to soothing music that helps you feel good.

For churchgoers, when music is playing at the beginning of service, they're setting the atmosphere. If you go to an event, they have music playing. The atmosphere is being established. So how are you regulating your atmosphere?

Recent research shows that listening to music improves our mental well-being and surprisingly boosts our physical health.

Music Makes You Happier

Research proves that your brain releases a "feel-good" neurotransmitter called dopamine when listening to music you like.

Unfortunately, stress can cause 60% of all our illnesses and diseases.

Listening to music, you enjoy decreased levels of the stress hormone cortisol in your body, which counteracts the effects of chronic stress.

Music Reduces Depression

Research demonstrates that music could benefit patients with depressive symptoms, depending on the type. For example, meditative sounds and classical music elevated people, but techno and heavy metal brought people down even more.

Music Elevates Your Mood While Driving

A study in the Netherlands discovered that listening to music can positively impact your mood while driving, leading to safer behavior.

Music Strengthens Learning and Memory

Researchers determined that music could help you learn and improve your recollection skills.

The third tool we recommend for your mind is spending time alone to eliminate outside distractions, especially when so much is happening around you.

There can be distractions coming in left, right and center from the news and people. You're absorbing other people's feelings, emotions, thoughts and ideas. However, when you spend time alone and you are still, you can hear God clearer. You can also listen to yourself and acknowledge your thoughts and feelings without interruptions from other things.

When you're alone, the break from external input helps you to rest and rejuvenate, allowing you to attract more positive things into your life. In addition, you remove the emotional noise created by the presence of others.

By experimenting with specific periods of solitude, you may begin to realize that you value social time a lot more. It may be partly maybe because you're grounded in a more profound sense of self, have plenty of time to prioritize yourself, and are less likely to feel resentful. Additionally, once you learn to enjoy being alone instead of fearing it, you will see that solitude allows you to pursue your most eccentric hobbies and authentic passions without compromising for anyone.

When you're with others, you naturally adjust aspects of yourself that you present to create a good rapport with these people, even if you're generally quite authentic. However, when you're alone, there's no one you need to please, and you get a clearer picture of the truth of who you are. This enhanced perspective on your identity helps you better figure out what would make you happy and what your life's purpose might be.

People who rarely spend time alone can feel quite panicked by the idea of being without others. This reliance leads to lower self-confidence.

If you're used to getting validation from others to feel good, you don't get much practice making yourself feel good. As a result, you may have a habit of looking outwards whenever you feel anxious or insecure.

Being alone helps you take a critical look at your self-talk. You learn how to offer yourself compassion and draw on your knowledge for confidence. Your self-esteem is how you see yourself. This view of yourself is influenced by many things like failures and successes of your past, statements people told you and the things you tell yourself. Words you speak to yourself every day have an immense impact on your subjective reality. If something seems unrealistic to you, it is unachievable.

Self-care for the body

Ensure that you're sipping on water throughout the day. Whether you're someone who believes in gulping it back at one time or sipping on one gallon throughout the day, our bodies are mostly water, so it needs constant replenishment.

The human body comprises around 60% water. Commonly, it's recommended that you drink eight 8-ounce glasses of water per day. Dehydration can have a noticeable effect if you lose as little as 2% of your body's water content, impairing many aspects of brain function and physical performance.

If you don't stay hydrated, your mental and physical performance can suffer.

We need to refresh ourselves to function. We need rest to reset. We can help the body by making sure we get enough sleep. Some of us are used to being on "team, no sleep - hustle, hard, play hard," but that shouldn't be the case anymore. Let's be one hundred percent team self-care.

You know it doesn't feel good when you don't get enough sleep. But you may not realize how far-reaching the impact can be.

Most adults need between seven and nine hours of sleep per day. Getting less than six or seven hours of sleep for just one night can affect you the next day, and chronically missing out on sleep increases your risk of disease.

During sleep, your body releases hormones. Some of them keep your heart and blood vessels healthy, while a lack of sleep deprives you of these hormones. These issues are all associated with high blood pressure, worsening heart function over time, and heart disease.

When you're sleep-deprived, your body releases stress hormones.

Stress can make you react in ways that aren't productive. For example, you may act out of fear or make rash decisions. Or you may be irritable. Likewise, a poor night's sleep can make you feel anxious.

Sleep also helps regulate your metabolism. That's the way your body converts food to energy. In addition, sleep regulates your immune system. Irregular immune system activity can cause inflammation when you don't get enough sleep. You may not notice excess inflammation, but it can affect your body.

Chronic inflammation damages structures and increases your risk of many health conditions.

A good night's sleep makes you feel energized and alert, which helps you focus and get things done. In addition, sleep is vital for memory formation, clear thinking, balance, and repairing damage from stress, ultraviolet rays, and other harmful exposures.

We don't realize how important it is to sleep. This team needs a minimum of seven hours and 20 minutes every night of sleep to function. So maybe for you, it could be eight hours, six hours, or nine hours. Whatever it is, make sure that you're getting enough sleep to help your body reset and restore.

The third thing for self-care for the body is staying physically active.

When we think about going through this present time, those emotions need to go somewhere for those struggling.

The health benefits of regular exercise and physical activity are hard to ignore. When you engage in physical activity, you burn calories. The more intense the movement, the more calories you burn. Physical activity stimulates various brain chemicals that may leave you feeling happier, more relaxed and less anxious.

Regular exercise helps prevent or manage many health problems and concerns, including:

- Stroke

- Metabolic syndrome

- High blood pressure

- Type 2 diabetes

- Depression

- Anxiety

- Many types of cancer

- Arthritis

It can also help improve cognitive function and help lower the risk of death from various causes.

Get moving. Healthy motion equals healthy emotion. So strive to get in 6000 to 10,000 steps a day. Being stagnant is the opposite of generating energy and keeping that vibration moving. Keep that energy moving because if we are not mobile, we sit in a slump with our emotions, not processing.

Self-care for the soul

Prayer helps a great deal. We feel like prayer is us having conversations with God. In meditation, you're still, listening for the answer and clearing the mind. Prayer and meditation can have a lot in common. Both can increase mindfulness and prevent excessive worry.

Praying within a relationship with God that feels loving and supportive may help manage stress and life's challenges. Prayer entails working through thoughts and circumstances. It also implies the context of a relationship with a higher being rather than existing on a solitary journey.

People pray for several reasons and specific outcomes. To share their angst and suffering in a relational context, show gratitude, and reflect. Studies have associated prayer with a sense of calmness, peace, encouragement or social support. Prayer can foster a sense of connection to a higher power, which people find important in life or their values. Prayer can reduce feelings of isolation, anxiety and fear as well.

The following tool for your soul is gratitude and affirmations. We strongly believe in actively practicing gratitude. We first learned about gratitude journaling from our mentor Bob Proctor when Makini decided to create *A Walk in My Stilettos: Gratitude Journal* to help others have a remarkable collection of their life's greatest moments.

We can say that we're grateful for something, but we gain more from actively, daily and intentionally practicing gratitude. When we do so, we're connecting to our feelings, We relate to how and why we feel the way we do about what we are grateful for. It positions us on a higher vibration.

If Makini is grateful for Suzana, why is she thankful for her? She's grateful for her support, love, and ability to co-create things. So when we connect the feeling to the things that we're thankful for, it helps shift our perspective and mind.

Gratitude does four things:

1. Gratitude disconnects us from toxic, negative emotions and the ruminating that often accompanies them.

2. Expressing gratitude helps us even if we don't explicitly share it with someone. We're happier and more satisfied with life.

3. The positive effects of written gratitude can compound like interest. You might overlook the benefit of a daily or weekly practice.

4. A gratitude practice trains the brain to be more in tune with experiencing gratitude — a positive plus a positive equals more positives.

There are many benefits to practicing gratitude, not limited to:

For the individual

- Increased happiness and positive mood

- More satisfaction with life

- Less materialistic

- Less likely to experience burnout

- Better physical health

- Better sleep

- Less fatigue

- Lower levels of cellular inflammation

- Greater resiliency

- Encourages the development of patience, humility and wisdom

For groups

- Increases prosocial behaviors

- Strengthens relationships

- May help employees' effectiveness

There is power in declaring things and speaking them into existence. As for affirmations, positive self-talk has made a significant difference in Makini's life, so she published a book about it. *A Walk In My Stilettos: 111 Affirmations to Help You Heal.*

Affirmations are more than motivational slogans. There is plenty of scientific evidence to show how and why affirmations work on your subconscious mind. There are even health benefits to using affirmations.

Most forms of psychological therapy or counseling are based on the idea that you can improve your mental health by changing your view of yourself. Meaning you can choose to see yourself as strong, intelligent and capable of doing whatever you want. And this is where affirmations that align with your values can be potent.

There is increasing research that shows the physical impact of affirmations on the structure of your brain. You introduce new concepts to your brain and open up new neural pathways when you practice positive affirmations. It helps to change your mindset from negative self-doubt to positive confidence.

Daily affirmations have a measurable impact on your resilience and how well you deal with stress. As well as having a positive effect on depression and anxiety, regular and consistent use of affirmations can help lower your levels of cortisol and adrenaline, both harmful stress hormones. As your stress response declines, your heart rate and blood pressure will decrease, reducing your stroke and heart attack risk. In addition, people who use affirmations are more likely to lead healthier lifestyles, exercise more and eat a healthy diet.

The third resource for the soul is having a community of healthy connections. Unfortunately, we don't give enough weight or appreciation to having healthy connections or having people around us who love and support us to help regulate our nervous system.

Healthy relationships are a vital component of health and well-being. There is compelling evidence that strong relationships contribute to a long, healthy and happy life. Conversely, the health risks from being alone or isolated in one's life are comparable to the risks associated with cigarette smoking, blood pressure and obesity.

Healthy connections can help you:

- Live longer

- Deal with stress

- Be healthier

- Feel richer

A lack of relationships can cause multiple physical, emotional, and spiritual health problems. The research is evident and devastating: **isolation is fatal.**

As people, we're constantly searching for connections. And when we have a healthy community of relationships, not only does that help us with our self-care, but it relieves us mentally. It helps to regulate us. And It helps by social proofing our lives when we can have conversations in safe spaces to connect. We are wired for connection. It is a biological imperative. A biological imperative is a need for living organisms to prolong their existence to survive.

We need it to survive. We've been in a global pandemic where we've been forced to isolate and be by ourselves, but we're not programmed that way.

Let's do a quick little exercise.

We invite you to take a moment and think about all the people around you, and we're going to put them into two main categories.

We connect with people for support, and to feel connected. And there may also be people that fall into both categories.

So, we want you to recollect the people constantly in your thoughts. Make a list of everyone in your inner circle. In what category would you place them? When you think of them, are they someone you connect with for support or someone that makes you feel a connection? Or is it both?

Who is in your social support network? Write a list of those people. Who do you feel socially connected to?

Let's cover these three questions and separate them on a scale of hardly ever, sometimes or often.

How often do you feel that you lack companionship? Hardly ever, sometimes or often?

How often do you feel left out? Hardly ever sometimes or often?

How often do you feel isolated from others? Hardly ever, sometimes or often?

Please review your answers. That will indicate what needs to be worked on because survival is dependent on opportunities to successfully co-regulate.

Your responses are going to let you know what areas need work.

How are you feeling today? What is the information telling you? What do you need to change?

We base our results in life on our actions, and our efforts are based on how we feel.

When we feel anxious, we're energetically out of alignment and are not in harmony with spirit. These feelings of uncertainty during the pandemic, with the weighted impact of everything transpiring, connect to our spiritual alignment. We will get more into the truth of who we are and our spiritual DNA.

Chapter 3:

Your Deeper Purpose

"Be still and know that I AM GOD."
Psalm 46:10 (English Standard Version)

The small things are so crucial daily. Meditation every day and just being still, quieting the mind is favorable. The discipline of even a five-minute consistent observance can create a focused, resilient, and aligned mindset.

Being still and connecting spiritually through prayer, meditation, or quieting the mind can bring the answers you need. The answers are always within you.

Where are you getting your support? How are you feeling right now? Acknowledge and honor where you're at now. We all go through periods where we may feel a little trapped or in a bit of a dip, or we might be experiencing some more profound challenges. Sometimes life might feel like it is a little too much to handle.

In Victor Frankl's book *Man's Search for Meaning*, he states that it is important to find meaning in suffering. During Frankl's experience as a prisoner in the concentration camp in Auschwitz, he found that those who had a '*why*' were significantly more likely to survive. During difficult times and challenges, those who lose faith, meaning, or hope and can connect to their deep *why* will find a way, even during the direst circumstances. Regardless of the condition, one finds themself.

So what is your 'WHY'?

What is your purpose?

Why are you here?

These essential questions help you connect with your core and driving force. Victor Frankl found his 'why' by documenting the events and having faith that one day when he was released from the camp, he would lecture about his experience. This thinking process helped him change the feeling of suffering into learning opportunities.

Is your WHY strong enough to get you through this challenging period?

Is your WHY strong enough to get you through anything?

Are you clearly and deeply connected to your meaning?

"Suffering ceases to be suffering the moment it finds meaning."

You must find a purpose bigger than yourself.

No matter the situation and how serious the challenge is, you always have a choice. As Victor Frankl profoundly pointed out, *"Anything can be taken from a person but the freedom to choose what they think."* No matter how complex your experience is, you have the freedom to choose your attitude. You have the freedom to decide how you react or respond to a situation. Your reactions or responses are based on your choice and the decision you have made at the moment. Every moment, you have a choice. At that moment, you can choose to complain, react or stay in misery or you can choose to respond by seeing the beauty, gratitude and opportunity in the situation.

So, how can you find meaning in difficulty, in your suffering? Remember, it is not about the situation. It's about your attitude within the situation that makes all the difference.

Living in a state of gratitude

We hear so much about "gratitude" these days. Messages like:

"Just be grateful."

"Keep a gratitude journal."

"Shouldn't you be grateful?"

Gratitude has become an *in* word. Everyone is talking about it, but not everyone is living by it. Before we go further, though, let us explain what gratitude is and what it does for you.

Gratitude is simply feeling the appreciation of any situation, person, or event in life. Remember, it is the feeling of appreciation that is most important. Giving genuine thanks from the heart creates a vibration that moves through the body, carried through you to the world.

Wallace D Wattles stated:

"The whole process of mental adjustment and attunement can be summed up in one word: gratitude."

Whatever your current situation is like, you can adjust how you feel by making gratitude a way of life. Like Viktor Frankl, changing an intensely bad experience into learning for his deeper purpose, gratitude can help transform any state of mind.

What are you grateful for right now, even though it may be a challenging time for you?

Gratitude is not about suppressing the more complex emotions. Therefore, it is important to honor your feelings. Let them move through you. You can feel the appreciation of your feelings at the same time. Or once you have allowed it to move through, you can assess what you are grateful for from the experience.

Intrinsically, we all want abundance. We believe this is because we were all born abundant and are fruitful. There is enough money, food, love, business, and joy in this world for everyone. So having wealth in every area of your life, including your health, relationships, finances, and home, is true abundance. And making gratitude your way of life will open you up to having a wealthy life.

There is plenty of information available about practicing gratitude, so these activities may not be new to you, but here are some ways you can express and feel your appreciation for everything. Remember, you must genuinely feel the gratitude you are expressing for it to have the impact and power it has in your life.

- Keep a gratitude journal - write down ten things every morning and evening about what you are thankful for in your life. If you want to go deeper, write down why you are grateful for this person, thing, or event.

- In the morning, spend five minutes sending love to someone you're feeling adverse energy from.

- Every hour on the hour, remind yourself what you are grateful for - you might want to set your alarm as a prompt to do this.

- Write a genuine thank you note to someone and explain why you appreciate them.

- Bless what you already have - even if you feel like you have a little bit of money, health, or love- bless it and be grateful for what you have.

- Tell people what you like about them.

- Meditate on the things you love and already have in your life.

- Pray from a state of feeling grateful and abundant.

Who do you think you are? The truth of YOU

Let us ask you a question.

Who do you think you are?

You see, whenever asked this question or when contemplated, it is common to think that you're your name, age and personality. For example, *I'm from a European background, living in Australia, born in Australia.* But that's not what we're trying to insinuate.

I am intelligent. I am not intelligent. I am in my forties. I am funny. I am not funny. I am this, and I am that. However, most of those are labels we've put on ourselves based upon experiences or interpretations of what we have experienced. We accept ideas and titles about who we are from society, family and childhood experiences.

So you may have grown up in a European migrant family where life was hard. Perhaps you felt that you had to study and follow a female role model behavior.

Or you may have had a trauma in your life. Maybe there was violence in your family growing up. Perhaps you grew up in a low-income family. So you subconsciously put a label on yourself that you can only get so far or that you can't have abundance.

Perhaps there was an experience at school. You may have had a bad day and failed a test, even though you were a child. And that was not a pleasant experience for you. So the teacher and your friends at school labeled you as 'not intelligent'. Possibly you said a joke, and someone laughed, which made you label your personality as funny.

Things happen, and then we create a label we follow and believe in for the rest of our lives. So you may have failed a test when you were a child. Even though your dream was to go to university and study to become something big, you felt that you were not good enough based on the ideas you accepted as your truth.

Let us ask you a question.

What if we were able to wipe all of those labels away?

And what if you were able to choose to be whomever you wanted to be and have whatever you wanted to have?

What if, inside yourself, you had infinite potential? Think about that. What's the definition of infinite? Don't just think about this with your head; open up. Open up your body, heart, and soul to receiving—'infinite' means that it continues forever and ever, and ever, and ever.

There's no end to the infinite. Right? So, what if this were true?

You see, the truth is that your spiritual DNA is perfect. Full stop. As our dear mentor, Bob Proctor, would say, "You have genius locked up inside you." You may feel it already on a deeper level. However, you're stuck with the thinking and programming that has always been— the same processing system you have had for years and for most of your life. Therefore, you choose to stay with the ideas of who you think you are rather than opening up to new ideas and the potential and possibility of who you could be.

Whatever you experienced as a child or growing up, whatever negative self-concept idea or label you are convinced is you, it is not.

So what if you accepted the idea that you have a well of infinite potential via the tiny seed planted inside.

What would accepting your truth about infinite potential change for you?

How would your life be different?

How would you be feeling about yourself right now?

What would you be doing differently?

Do you see? Let's back that up…

It is not just a belief. It is knowing. You know why— it's because we have used this information to change our lives. We've tapped into our inner potential to change our lives, and we can help you change yours too. But not only that, there is scientific evidence that this is true.

It might be the first time you have heard what we are about to share with you, or you may have heard it many times but have not yet allowed it to sink in. No matter how many times you have or have not heard this, we invite you to open up your mind, body and heart to receive the truth about yourself. And if it goes over your head, that's okay. Keep reading and opening up to what we are about to share with you; allow it to sink in. Once you have deeply accepted this truth, your life will pivot and change.

According to Dr. Joe Dispenza, in his book, *You Are the PLACEBO*, research in quantum physics studies the tiniest particles and how they interact to create the world we live in. It shows that when the tiniest part of the atom, the nucleus, was researched, the closer they looked, the less distinct the atom became until they could not see it at all. From these studies, atoms appear to be 99.999999999999% space. When they looked deeper into the space, they found that it was not empty at all, but it was filled with energy. Moreover, it was filled with a broad range of frequencies that make up an invisible, interconnected information field.

Dr. Joe Dispenza continues to explain that if every atom is 99.99999999999% energy or information, then everything that we know to exist in the universe is really just energy and information. No matter how solid or condensed the object.

This energy or information is actual intelligence. It is related to the same intelligence that is omnipresent, omnipotent, and that has created everything that exists in the world and the entire universe. Some like to refer to this intelligence as God/source intelligence.

That is a fascinating fact, but what does this mean about you?

It means that you, our friend, are 99.99999999999% source intelligence. You may have thought that you are a physical being with a spirit. However, you are actually less physical (only .0000001% physical). You are a spiritual/energetic being having a physical experience.

The person you were saying you think you are and the labels you have put on yourself are not true. The paradigms you hold and carry about yourself are less than 1% (closer to zero percent) truth. And this is a scientific fact. So regardless if you continue to believe the labels that keep you limited or not, the reality is that you are limitless.

Imagine you are focused one hundred percent of the time on yourself, which is less than 1% of the truth of who you are. So what is this? 99.99999999999%. It is pure infinite intelligence. What does that mean? It is the energy that has created stars, galaxies, and planets, and it has created you. It's made everything that we see.

This is universal energy. It's the highest form of intelligence. It's God, and that's the truth of who you are. You are not your limits. You may be experiencing a difficult time right now. Many people are, but you are not who you thought you were. When you realize that, you become pure potential power. You can tap into the same energy inside yourself that has created the stars, galaxies, and universes - your inner genius. The universe is infinite and so are you.

You can choose to stay stuck in what's happening in your life and continue to live with the same old patterns where nothing much really changes. Or you could decide to tap into the power, the genius and the truth of who you are. By choosing to do so, you are tapping into your infinite potential. And this is where you begin to tap into new, adventurous and limitless possibilities.

Before we move on, we discuss one more thing, using Suzana's background as an example. Suzana always had big dreams. She always wanted to do what she's doing now as a career. Suzana always wanted to become a best-selling author since she was a kid. But as far as she can remember, there were always blocks.

Suzana would achieve some level of success, and she did very well in a senior management role. She had an above-average pay, but it wasn't for her. There was a bigger purpose on the horizon. In 2017, Suzana met Makini Smith in Toronto, and she was already a published author. Makini had attractive, quiet confidence. Being Proctor Gallagher Institute Consultants, they were both attending training with their mentor, Bob Proctor, who only recently passed away.

If you don't know who Bob Proctor was, he was the most significant leader in human potential in recent times. Bob Proctor was a world-renowned speaker, motivational coach, author of bestselling books, and a Law of Attraction teacher. He was featured in the documentary *The Secret* and had an international reputation for getting the very best out of helping people and businesses tap into their potential.

Suzana was at the front of that room, in front of Bob. He said something that resonated with every single cell in her body.

It went right through her like anything she'd ever experienced before. So let's revisit his words while we invite you to open up to the same idea. He said,

"Did you know that the entire universe would be out of alignment if you did not exist?"

WOW! Think about that - If **you** did not exist, the whole universe would be out of alignment. If you haven't fallen off your chair, you haven't absorbed the meaning of that statement yet. Let's repeat it.

Without you, the entire universe would be out of alignment.

What does that mean? Think about it. The whole universe. It is source energy, the energy from which everything that we know exists has been created.

The energy is God energy. And if you did not exist, the universe would not be able to function the way it's operating right now— without you. There would be an essential piece of the puzzle missing, and nothing in the universe would be able to function on an even keel— if your spiritual DNA did not exist. Open up to the truth of who you are because one thing we know for sure, we can say that you've been playing small.

Like most people, you are living in a prison cell and probably haven't been aware of it. Your cell is composed of walls that are your labels and self-imposed limiting thoughts. The key to unlocking the door to your prison cell lies in letting go of those false limits and tapping into your truth. How would your life change if you were able to live from that space of truth every day rather than live from your false lies, labels, paradigms and viruses in your mind of who you thought you were? Once you accept that you are 99.9999999999% intelligence and source energy and less than 1% physical, you can let go of the prison into freedom.

What is true freedom?

True freedom is tapping into your innate power to create the life you want to live every day. You understand that creation happens inside you because you are a creative force. After all, you are God's highest form of design. This is true freedom because no matter your current life's physical situation, you understand that you have the power to change it. And when you know the highest form of creation is you - you start to tap into infinite possibilities that you have never imagined possible for yourself in the past. As God's highest form of creation, you are the most powerful creative force that exists.

We hear all the time that God created us in his image.

Therefore, that means our spiritual DNA is perfect. However, we allow the viruses of doubt, worry and fear to interfere with the vision of our lives. We hope you realize how important you are, how vital your actions are, how much you matter, your stories matter, your life matters, and its impact.

We want you to take a moment to think. As people, we think in pictures. The whole world operates on images. Every time we talk about anything, we're using words or gestures to create a story and a specific image in someone else's mind or our minds. So think about your mental representation for your greatest life. Contemplate your vision for your life now that you have opened up your mind to infinite possibilities.

What would it look like?

What would you like it to be?

Who would you be if you weren't focusing on self-doubt, worry, fear, and all of those viruses?

If you were honing in on your truth and your greatness, what would you love your life to look like?

What vision do you have for yourself?

Think in as clear a picture as you possibly can.

Where in the world would you love to live?

What would that look like?

Would it be a house?

Would it be an apartment?

Would it be a lakefront property?

What does that look like for you?

What impact would you love to be making in the world?

What would you do every day?

If you had a choice, because we do, if there were no obstacles, what would you like the life for your child(ren) to look like?

What kind of car would you love to drive?

Where would you love to travel?

How often would you travel?

Create that vision for your life. People always talk about creating vision boards, but they're doing it backwards. They're opening up a magazine and cutting out pretty pictures and pasting them onto a board and not connecting with their deep inner vision for their life. What would you love your life to look like? You need first to know the vision you have for your life. That way, when you go to the magazine, you know what is specifically connected to your truth.

How would you love it to be if there were no obstacles? Take the time to write out the picture of what that vision looks like for you because you have more power and control than you realize. We often don't set specific goals or have clear visions, allowing things to just happen. We're letting "chance" rule our lives rather than ourselves using our innate power to create the life we would love to live.

You have power. You can create the life you desire. You need to create the vision for what you are yearning to have. Use your imagination. We need to be very specific about what we want. If we're not providing any instructions, we get whatever comes our way. God is a God of order.

Our environment is a reflection of what is happening in our minds. It's a looking glass into the image we have for ourselves.

The most well-known universal law out of all twelve is the law of attraction. Like attracts like, so whether it's negative or positive, everything you see in your life is what you've attracted. You attract everything in your life through the energy from the words you speak to your beliefs. You can even attract people into your life who have the same energy frequency as you.

Everything we do is based on universal law because it works one hundred percent of the time. If you were to drop a penny, what would happen? Would it rise? No. Would it float? No. Do we not know what's going to happen? Does something different happen during this time? Every single time, it drops—right? It works a hundred percent of the time, even if you are ignorant of the law behind it.

So if a baby was standing on a balcony five floors high, and it falls because it leans over and drops, the law of gravity is not going to say, 'Oh, it's a baby.' It's ignorant. It's innocent. It will not float until mom comes or someone comes and saves it. It will fall.

The first universal law is order. God, the universe, that infinite intelligence inside you requires you to lead the way. It requires you to imagine an image what you want, and holding onto that image will then change your vibration. Then that vibration, which is also an emotion, will lead you into action, but you will also start to attract what you want. So the first step is to know what you want. Now that you know the whole universe would be out of alignment without you, what would you love? What would you love instead?

Fear and faith are both beliefs in the unknown. We have the ability to choose. It's about believing. We can believe and be afraid of not being able to do something or fearful of what will happen, or we can choose to accept and have faith that it will happen.

It's that energy, that vibration, that opens you to receive those things. We often talk about external factors and people blocking our blessings when sometimes it's us. Sometimes we do just that with our thoughts.

With the uncertainty and chaos going on in the world, our nervous system is constantly being triggered. We need to explore ways to self-regulate. Some of us have experienced past traumas that have programmed our approach away from connection toward protection. In a state of preservation, survival is the only goal. The system is closed to connection and change. In a connective state, health, growth and restoration are possible.

Suzana will lead us in a meditation to calm the nervous system, which helps program our system toward safety and connection.

Heart-centered meditation

Make sure you're comfortable. For example, you might be sitting in your chair or lying down flat on your back. If you're sitting in your chair, make sure your feet are flat on the ground.

Ensure that you're completely comfortable and supported in your chair. Do not cross your legs or your arms. Now, close your eyes for a few moments.

Any thoughts that come up, anything that may be bothering you—it's okay. Let's put it aside for a few minutes and be present and in the moment.

Let's sit in silence in stillness and relax your toes, feet, and beautiful feet. They've carried you all of your life. They've walked through dark periods with you. They danced during joyful celebrations. They've helped you run and ride a bike. They carry you through every single day.

Just focus on your feet. Allow them to relax completely.

The tops and bottoms of your feet are completely relaxed.

Relax your ankles, your shins, your calves, completely relaxed. Now, your knees, your thighs, all the way to your buttocks, your pelvis, completely relaxed. Your pelvis is your creative center.

Just allow it to relax.

Relax your stomach, your solar plexus. Your chest, relax. Relax your lower back, your middle back, your shoulders. Completely relax. Your upper arms, elbows, forearms, and wrists, and feel the relaxation moving into both of your beautiful, beautiful hands and moving through the top and bottom of your hand to your fingertips.

Let's focus on every single finger on both hands, including your thumb, completely relaxed.

Let go and feel the relaxation. Relax your neck and your throat. Just allow your throat to relax. Your voice is so important. You have a voice. Relax your jaw and your cheeks. Relax the intricate muscles around your mouth, nose and eyes. Now, notice the muscles around your eyes and just completely relax. Relax your forehead, your temples—just completely relax.

Now, take a few deep breaths in and then let go. From the top of your head, the side of your head, the back of your head. Now your whole body is completely relaxed as you let go. Beautiful.

Breathing in and letting it all go.

Now, take your awareness to the center of your chest. Let's take it to your heart. Just be. Feel the energy in the center of your heart. This is a sacred space.

Feel the stillness, and ultimately allow yourself to experience the present moment.

Open up your heart center to the message and the truth of who you are. The fact is that without you and your beautiful aura, the whole universe would be out of alignment. It could not exist the way it does now, nor could it function without you opening up from your heart, preparing to let everything in. So stay with this beautiful part of the peace, the joy, the gratitude and the space from your heart center.

What would your heart center love? Your heart knows that you are limitless. Experience this knowledge from this center.

That feeling? Hold on to it. Everything else, let it go. There's nothing you need to do right now. Just feel it from your heart center. You have genius inside you. It's unlocked now that you know the truth.

From this state of being, ask yourself, what would I love? How would you love to feel about yourself? What would you love for your life right now?

You are of infinite life. The usual endless love for everything you want and need is inside you.

Now, let's bring up the feeling of gratitude from your heart. Hold on to the gratitude for anything you want to feel gratitude for right now. Think of the gratitude for the challenges, too, because you wouldn't be able to learn and stretch without them. Focus on it for yourself and the life you are meant to have.

I am so profoundly grateful to co-create with my beautiful, soul-sister Makini. I'm also so grateful to have the honor to lead you all into this space today. Thank you. When you're ready, open your eyes.

How are you feeling after that meditation?

It's one thing for us to inspire you and bring these things to your awareness, but it's entirely another for you to take action. So what we're going to challenge you to do is take some time to create the vision you want for your life and yourself. It is time to write it out—a full description in the present tense.

If you're not someone who writes, record it on your cell phone. Create a detailed voice note of what that vision looks like for your life.

The action is where the results come in. Now, this is your opportunity to take action and take steps towards your vision and the results you want for your life.

We hope you really felt blessed through this exercise, and it created an impact on you. Today, we hope you've opened up even a little bit to what's available to you.

Please write down what came through for you during that meditation.

Chapter 4:

Overcoming Your Fears

"Courage is fear walking."
— Susan David

We took time to honor the present and acknowledge our feelings because they are valid. They are data.

We learned that our spiritual DNA is perfect and how the world would not be the same without you.

We learned that we are wired for connection.

We had a beautiful guided meditation to calm our nervous system.

We created our vision for our life.

What was your "A-HA" moment?

We are now going to learn about overcoming our fears and the terror barrier. Then we will discuss how you can break through and receive the rewards waiting for you on the other side.

We often ask ourselves how to overcome our fears. But, genuinely believe the courage and resilience of strong qualities people admire are part of the quiet, shy woman walking in her fear. Courage is fear walking. It exists, but you learn how to work through it. Repeatedly working at it builds the resilience muscle.

Fear itself is not the real problem. Our problem is that we fear the wrong thing. What we should fear are the missed opportunities fear presents. We are the only ones responsible for our present limitations in life.

Many of us are holding ourselves back. Sometimes we attempt to shift blame and say that other people are blocking our blessings. But still, we don't realize that we can hinder our prayers because we allow fear, doubt, worry and negative self-talk and all those low vibrational things to hinder us from reaping the rewards and beauty that life offers.

It's a painful realization. It isn't easy to look in the mirror and own how we have participated in the self-sabotage. It's sad and hard to swallow, but we have to learn to acknowledge our contributions to our circumstances rather than blame others. The faster we own it and take responsibility, the sooner we can take action and move forward.

Makini used to fear flying on airplanes, but presently, she loves to travel. She would refuse any flights over four hours because that was the longest Makini could bear the experience of panic attacks, anxiety and motion sickness. Her parents lived in two different countries after their marriage dissolved as a child. They would put her on a flight with airline supervision to Jamaica, having her fly from where she resided in Canada with her mother to Jamaica, where her father lived. Makini was terrified.

As she grew older, dreams of seeing the world were a hurdle, and she avoided flying as much as possible. When Makini started flourishing in personal development, and was blessed with opportunities to speak, coach and do book signings worldwide, she could have allowed the fear of flying to paralyze her. Makini refused to let it stop her from going after the things she wanted or making the impact that she sought to make. She could have easily turned down the presented opportunities that she once prayed for.

Why block the blessings?

She had to learn to move through the fears. Moving through that barrier of fear allowed her to experience trips to South Africa, Paris, Amsterdam, Puerto Rico, and more. The abundance of international book signings, global clients and the beauty of seeing parts of the world have been the gift that keeps on giving.

The key is getting to the root of the problem.

Why are you procrastinating?

What do you fear?

Why are we not moving forward?

The reason typically connects to something we fear.

There's an acronym for fear, F. E. A. R. It initially states false evidence appearing real.

F. E. A.R is an acronym for :

False

Evidence

Appearing

Real

After the opportunity to connect with Bob Proctor and other thought leaders presented itself, it opened up her mind to what is possible. We need to learn and get out of our own way. The experience led to Makini renaming the acronym. So now, let's look at it from a different perspective: face everything and rise.

F. E. A.R is also:

FACE

EVERYTHING

AND

RISE

We can no longer see it as false evidence appearing real because the realization that everything you've ever wanted is on the other side of what you fear. So why would you stay in a dark mental place, afraid to go after things you desire or your purpose? Instead, like Makini, you could push through that fear and reap the rewards. Most times, the rewards are not monetary or tangible things. It's simply about the gratifying feeling.

Being a mindset coach, social media influencer and public speaker, most people don't believe Makini when she says she's the typical, severe introvert. Introverts tend to be more quiet, reserved, and reflective. Unlike extroverts who gain energy from social interaction, introverts have to expend energy in social situations. After attending a party or spending time in a large group of people, introverts often need to recharge by spending time alone.

Makini's extreme shyness and need to be alone used to get in her way. She was afraid of public speaking and fearful of conversations with a stranger. Social events and networking drained her energy to the point of needing an entire day in bed afterwards to recover.

If Makini had held on to that fear of public speaking, she wouldn't be doing any of the things she is doing today that she deeply enjoys. She wouldn't be making the impact and coaching and speaking to women's organizations empowering them to walk in their greatness. Makini would not feel a connection with people from around the world. If she stayed in that place of fear, she wouldn't be living the lifestyle she is living today, a life of purpose and leaving a long-lasting legacy.

When Makini was in the sixth grade, she was asked to deliver a class speech, and her teacher loved it so much that she requested that Makini share it at the school assembly. Standing in the front of the auditorium before the entire school, she froze, standing there like a statue and couldn't move. She couldn't deliver her speech, much less finish it. Makini looked out at hundreds of her schoolmates, and the thought of messing up caused her to panic and shut down. After a few minutes, a teacher eventually rescued her from further embarrassment and ushered her back to her seat, where Makini tried to disappear into the glossy hardwood floors.

Due to that experience, Makini has been terrified of public speaking ever since. She has since learned an actual term for this—glossophobia. The fear of public speaking is surprisingly common. Experts estimate that as much as 77% of the population has anxiety regarding public speaking. Of course, many people can manage and control the fear. However, suppose your fear is significant enough to cause problems in work, school, or social settings. In that case, you may have a full-blown phobia.

You've probably heard that public speaking is feared more than death itself. Makini is one of the people that fall into that category. However, connecting with Bob Proctor, his wife Linda, and his daughter, Colleen Proctor, helped her work through that fear of public speaking.

They were at an event, and Bob Proctor's wife, Linda, got up to the front of the room to introduce some of the other people she worked alongside. She had said Makini's name and asked her to get up and introduce herself. She didn't realize her inside voice projected loudly and said, "Oh, crap." She was terrified to have all of the attention on her.

After that meeting, Bob Proctors' daughter, Colleen, approached her and said, "You know, we need to work on that. What is it that you're terrified of?"

She was focused on the energy of what people were thinking of her or how she was being perceived. Makini was more focused on all of the energy that was coming her way.

"Makini, you have so much value in you," she said. "You have a message to share. You have a fantastic story. You can make such a significant impact. Instead of focusing the energy on yourself, take everything you have inside to share and know that it is of value. Focus on what you have to give and put that energy out."

That helped shift Makini's perspective on her fear of public speaking. Sometimes we have to look at the root of our fear. The source of fear is usually self-doubt. We procrastinate when we encounter it, but you don't have to remove self-doubt to start. Starting or action eliminates the doubt. Doubt removes action.

There are many reasons why we fear certain things, but when you start to look at these obstacles and where they're coming from, you can dig deeper to address what's causing you to procrastinate.

There are six reasons why people will typically procrastinate.

Six Reasons why people procrastinate:

1. Boredom

2. Annoyance

3. Difficulty

4. Ambiguous

5. Unstructured

6. Lacks purpose

So ask yourself, why are you procrastinating? Which of the six things is causing you to procrastinate?

Think of a situation right now. Something that you are procrastinating on. Which of the six things is the trigger for what you're currently procrastinating from doing? Next, think about your present, something that you are afraid to do that's causing you to procrastinate. If something is boring, what's a way that you can make it exciting?

Maybe it's a task or a job that you feel lacks purpose. How can you give it meaning?

If it's something that feels unstructured, how can you create the structure to help you work through your fear or procrastination of getting through that thing?

Do the opposite of the challenge by taking action! If it's difficult, why is it difficult? How can you make it easy? What action do you need to take to make it easy?

It doesn't have to take you ten years to reach that one year that will change your life.

Again, here are the six reasons.

One, it could be boring.

Two, it could be annoying.

Three, it could be difficult.

Four, it could be ambiguous.

Five, it could be unstructured.

And six, it can be something that lacks purpose.

Suzana loves public speaking, but it has not always been easy. Like Makini shared in her story of when she was a child, Suzana felt that she had no voice because of a lot of trauma. So, somewhere at a very early age, she learned that she could not voice her opinion or speak up.

Anytime she expressed something or spoke to someone with authority, she felt paralyzed with fear. Suzana is one of those people who would freeze. So public speaking did not come naturally.

About four years ago, in senior management, she was highly experienced. Then, while in a room with superiors in an interview, she completely froze. Another time, she was presenting, and even to this day, it's embarrassing to think about, she completely froze. But fear is nothing to put yourself down about. Even the most successful, including Bob Proctor, whom we all admire, would have stories of the impacts and his experience with fear.

Often, when we feel fear and make mistakes like that, we feel a little bit humiliated. Suzana undoubtedly felt humiliated, freezing twice while in senior management. It overwhelmed her. She didn't know what to do about it and felt like she had failed somehow.

She had carried that emotion for so long. But really, fear is a part of your growth. What we think is a failure is a part of success. As mentioned, every one of us, even the most successful person, would have stories where they felt that their fear took over.

We remember Bob Proctor saying that, even to this day, he is faced with a bit of fear when he has a lofty goal. So, we will share with you a diagram that the Proctor Gallagher Institute (PGI) uses and that we use in our valuable coaching sessions. It shows you the stages of what happens to you when you go through fear, and by understanding these stages, you're able to break through to the other side.

If you're not feeling fear in pursuing your dream, it means that you're comfortable. You're not growing. As Susan Jeffers said, "Feel the fear and do it anyway." In pursuing your dream, you must feel the fear and move through it. And on the other side of fear lies growth and a powerful part of you that you have not experienced before.

So let's go through the stages of fear.

UNDERSTANDING

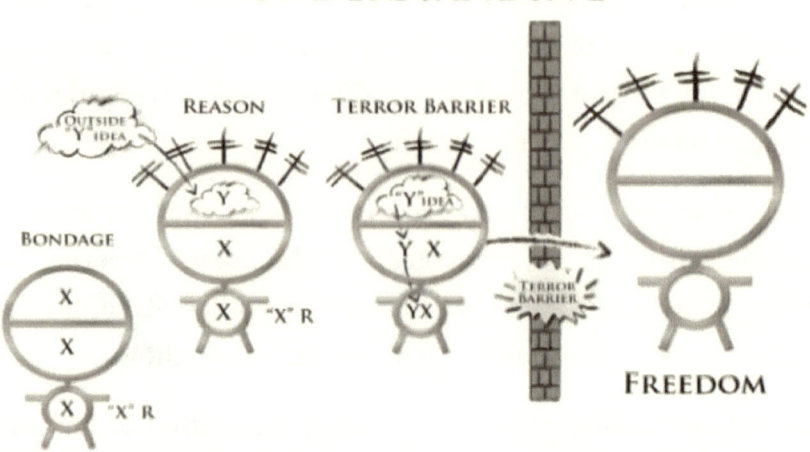

Diagram 1. The 4 Stages of the Terror Barrier from PGI's Thinking Into Results Participants Guide

The little circle represents your body. In the big circle, you can see that the mind is divided into two parts. The top part represents your conscious mind, and the bottom part represents your subconscious mind.

Your conscious mind represents 5% of your thinking. Your conscious mind is your logical mind—your thinking mind. It is where you process information, analyze, experience the five senses and where you imagine.

Your subconscious mind controls 95% of your thoughts, feelings, behaviors and results in every area of your life. Your subconscious mind, on the other hand, is your emotional mind. The part of your mind controls your beliefs, skills, habits, reactions, attitudes, behavior, habitual thoughts, and deeply embedded feelings.

Suppose you start to understand how your subconscious works. In that case, you begin to understand why your life has been the way it has and why you may feel blocked or frustrated about achieving, having, or experiencing something you really want.

There is so much in your subconscious controlling your results at the moment. So if you feel paralyzed by fear when you step out of your comfort zone or your habitual way of thinking and behaving, know that this is your subconscious.

Something happens, and it automatically triggers the same thoughts, feelings, behavior and results. It is your automatic response. These are called your subconscious paradigms. A paradigm is a habitual way of thinking and behaving, and most of our behaviors are habitual. So to break through and start to achieve better results in your life, you must change your paradigms.

Your conscious mind represents the mind that you see images with, the mind that interprets your five senses. It's your rational mind. It is your thinking mind. So to read this book, your conscious mind is doing the thinking and the analyzing.

Did you know that your subconscious processes 40 million pieces of information every single minute? Most of which you are not aware of? Your subconscious is automatic.

So, what does that mean? You are walking around unconsciously or subconsciously every day. You think that you're thinking, but you're really not. Now, what does that mean when you are experiencing fear? Earlier, we stated that fear is necessary. It's a part of your growth. So above in Diagram 1, there are four stick person drawings.

In order to break through the fear or the terror barrier, according to Proctor Gallagher Institute, there are four stages that one goes through.

Breaking through the Terror Barrier

The four stages of moving through fear are according to Proctor Gallagher Institute's Thinking Into Results program:

1. Bondage

2. Reason

3. Terror Barrier

4. Freedom

Bondage

Bondage is when your thoughts, feelings, behaviors, and results remain the same as they have always been. Both conscious and subconscious minds are congruently vibrating on the frequency of what you have always known. They are not challenged.

An example of this would be someone earning $60,000 per year, having been in the same job with the same company earning the same salary for years and years. That person never thought there could be better opportunities and might not have even tried. As a result, they live their life based on earning $60,000 per year and never look outside the box for any other possibility. Let's say that their conscious and subconscious mind is operating on an "X" vibration.

As long as this person does not entertain any other idea or possibility for themselves, they stay in the "X" vibration and will ultimately remain to earn a salary of $60,000 per year.

As soon as they start entertaining another idea, they move out of bondage into the second stage of the terror barrier. For example, this person's boss approached them one day and encouraged them to go for a new position with more responsibility and a salary of $100,000.

Initially, the person in bondage may think that this is not for them, and they don't entertain the idea of more, so nothing changes. But let's say the boss encourages them more and more, and one day they start to think, "I wonder what it would be like if I did earn $100,000?" If I earned $100,000, I could have that home or car or pay off my mortgage and travel.

So they are starting to entertain new ideas about what is possible for them. As soon as this happens, the person has entered the second stage of the terror barrier, called "reason."

Reason

The next stage of fear is reason —when the person starts to use their conscious mind to develop a new idea. They might begin to think about what they would be doing with the money, the new role and how they would show up. This person starts to create a new image of what is possible. This unique image and possibility vibrate at a different frequency. Let's just call it the "Y" frequency.

Nothing changes if they don't get emotionally involved in the new idea. So there is the "Y" frequency in the conscious mind while the subconscious continues to stay with the old vibration or frequency called "X."

As soon as the person starts to get emotionally involved with the new idea of earning $100,000 per year - they might become excited or feel a deep desire to have it. Then, the third stage is entered, called "the terror barrier."

Terror Barrier

The third stage, called the terror barrier, is where the discomfort and fear really kick in. Fear often overwhelms the individual. Some have never explored this possibility for themselves. However, now that the individual has become emotionally involved with this new idea, they want to have it, yet they are afraid and uncomfortable. In most cases, rather than breaking through into the freedom of living their dream, the discomfort is so intense that they let go of their new possibility and go back to their comfort zone of stage one, bondage.

To help you break through, let's explain why this happens. During the stage of the terror barrier, your conscious mind is vibrating at the new "Y" frequency. You vibrate here because of the depth of emotional involvement of the dream that has seeped into your subconscious mind. However, your subconscious is also in the same old "X" vibration (what you have always known), so you have the conflicting pulse of "X" and "Y" in your subconscious.

When you comprehend what is happening on the subconscious level, you understand that it is the conflict of vibration. You can and will break through the terror barrier by calming down the fear, connecting deeper to your dream and taking action to move towards it even though it is uncomfortable. Remember, the terror barrier is necessary for your growth.

Freedom

Freedom is the fourth and final stage of the terror barrier. It is when you have broken through the fear and now have a new paradigm in your mind. You have grown, and you no longer fear your dream.

When you become comfortable with your new result, for example, let's say the person in the example above takes action to go for the new position promoted by their boss. They successfully win the job and now earn $100,000 per annum. Eventually, this will become their new routine and comfort zone. So, therefore, the individual will be at stage one of the terror barrier again, which is bondage. To keep stretching and growing, we need to keep identifying with new possibilities and bigger dreams.

There's growth. The great thing about evolving is, yes, that's where we can enjoy more of our successes. But the best thing about it is that it's not all about the money or the title. It's not about being in the top 1% of the Proctor Gallagher Institute consultants. It is about the person that you become. Every time you breakthrough that terror barrier and move closer to your dream, you experience a part of yourself that you did not even know lived. You have jewels stored within that no money can buy.

You start to experience gems and diamonds and the most priceless gifts. You will never find these gifts on the outside. They are lying dormant within, waiting for you to transform. Like Joseph Campbell's quote: *"The cave you fear to enter holds the treasure that you seek."*

Remember, everything is a vibration, everything. You are more a source of intelligence or energy than you are physical. Remind yourself of this when experiencing the terror barrier and connect to your spirit. It will help move you past your fear.

Remind yourself that fear is a lower vibration than love, desire and your spirit. So, what do you need to do? Increase your vibration. Feel the fear, and at the same time, get excited about your goal and what you can contribute. Get enthusiastic about yourself because you have something to offer the world that nobody else can.

Flip the lower vibration of the fear. It may still be there, but you can also change it to excitement. It is easier to keep moving through the terror barrier and into your freedom when you understand that.

We could flip it to excitement because our bodies feel anxiety and excitement as the same feeling. It's all just about our perspective and how we choose to look at it.

It's all about perspective. Makini went from a girl with a fear of public speaking to a woman excited to speak and empower others to find their voice. She's excited to share and support others in their journey.

Usually, when we have severe changes in our lifestyle, we run up against the terror barrier. That is us coming out of our comfort zone. So many of us get imposter syndrome when we step out of what we know. We feel like we don't belong because we're in the vibration at the terror barrier wall. We have the opportunity to choose to return to comfort and not reap the rewards. The masses will do this because our brains are programmed for safety. Or, we can push through that wall, through the terror barrier, to receive those rewards.

Like many things that Makini and Suzana have both achieved, they were terrified at first. However, they felt the fear and did it anyway. It was walking in that fear that resulted in courage. Moving through that terror barrier is where they built up confidence. When you do the thing you fear to do, the feeling is gratifying. You realize that the actual action was less fearful than the fear itself. It's going through those experiences where we build up our confidence. It is built through your competence. So, your confidence increases in doing what you fear and then doing it repeatedly. At this point, it no longer feels as though it's as hard as it once was thought to be.

Something that you once may not have been able to do because you were afraid to push through that terror barrier and get to the other side when you do it. You will then understand that you can do anything you put your mind to. It is not as challenging as we thought it would have been. That is where the rewards start to appear.

What is a present situation you are afraid of?

Think deeply. What is something that you may be presently avoiding? Maybe it's work-related. Perhaps it's personal.

Think of something you have been afraid to do. Maybe it could be traveling, or perhaps it could be public speaking. Possibly it could be something as simple as having a challenging conversation with a family member.

It's simply comprehension. Once we understand, we know that we come out of bondage by taking action. Once we are aware, we can reap the rewards and get to the other side where the blessings are.

If you knew that you had the talent, ability and resources required to accomplish something beyond what you were currently working on, what would that be?

Often we're afraid to go after things because we're looking at all the obstacles. Instead of getting in harmony with the vibration, we're looking at everything in the way. So, our wants/desires exist at a higher vibration, and we're just hovering below it at a lower vibration.

What would bring you up higher to the goal you want, that thing you want, whatever that reward is for your life? If you removed the doubt, fear, and the negative self-talk you could possess—what is that thing?

Could you list all of the what-ifs? What would your life be like if you pushed through the fear to accomplish that goal?

Make a grocery list of all the things that could happen. Now get emotionally involved with it. We're going to make that your imagined reality. And because the fear does exist, and we push through it, sometimes we can acknowledge it if we know what the fears are. Rather than being caught off guard, we can plan for the worst, so we are not allowing those things to hold us back.

Make a list of your doubts, fears, and worries to know they exist. You know they're there, but you're going to push through. Look at your fears and write out what you're going to do about them. We're going to break through that terror barrier.

The action. All the results reside in taking action.

So think of that situation that you're afraid of and respond to the following:

1. If you knew you had all the talent, ability and resources required to accomplish something beyond what you are working on, what would that goal be?

2. List as many what-ifs as you can regarding your life if you accomplished this goal.

3. Now, become emotionally involved. Let it be part of your imagined reality.

4. List your fears, doubts and worries.

5. Look at your fears and write down what you will do about them to move forward. Stop procrastinating to reap all the rewards that life has for you. Open yourself up to the blessings that are there for you.

Choose one thing that you're going to take action on.

Do you remember the four stages of the terror barrier? Once you're in the terror barrier, what can occur if you don't take action?

You go back to bondage, and every time you go back to bondage, you start to lose a tiny little bit of yourself. Just a tiny bit. And what do I mean by that? Remember, you are destined for greatness. Infinite potential resides inside you. That thing that you so desire, that's in your heart, that thing that we felt, you felt during the meditation earlier—that is meant to be.

Dig deep. Every time you do not take action and move back into bondage, you think, 'Oh, forget about it. I'll just stay in this job. I won't go for it. I don't have the money. It's not the right time.' So every time you don't face your fears, you live a life of bondage that might be comfortable but progressive.

You also lose a little bit of courage and a little bit of confidence. So we're not going to leave you with just this information. We are not only here to share information, but we also want you to live your best life. So we're going to ask you to choose one thing that will move you towards the life you would love.

And you're going to take action in the next forty-eight hours.

Taking immediate action is a great way to remedy your fear.

Chapter 5:

Goal Setting

"Your goals are the roadmap that show you what's possible for your life."
— Les Brown

How true it is. Without a burning desire to achieve something great or worthy of your precious life, you are likely to drift through life and allow circumstances to control you.

How many people do you know who are excited about waking up in the morning? Or who genuinely loves their life and what they do? But unfortunately, far too many people live their lives in a deep state of misery - they are in jobs that they don't enjoy, relationships that aren't fulfilling, and often feel stuck and maybe a little overwhelmed in debt.

The misery that adults feel in western society today is far too prevalent. But, it is not supposed to be that way. Life should be as exciting as it once was as a child, if not even more exciting. Life was never meant to live in misery. Today, more and more adults are accumulating debt, believing that the new house, car or wardrobe will fill the void they are feeling inside. Yet, they soon find out that the hole only gets more significant, and every time they purchase a fix, they need a bigger one to fill the never-ending and growing space inside of them.

Although material wealth is lovely, it is fantastic to be abundant, which can undoubtedly add to the quality of your life. But when you create further debt that adds to stress and pressure, you are creating more debt if you purchase more things to fill the void. Therefore, it will not solve anything.

True abundance comes from within. You must fill up your heart and mind with joy, appreciation, and a strong foundation before you can bask in true material wealth and love every minute of it.

One of the reasons why adults are not showing up and living their best lives is because:

1. They are not connected to a deeper purpose.

2. They are not deeply connected to a goal or dream that is bigger than them.

We have already covered the importance of having a purpose so let's look at having a profound goal or dream. We have goals to stretch and grow us into becoming more of who we were created to be. Having a goal or dream that is so big that you have never achieved it before can be frightening. However, not being entirely sure how you will achieve it is a critical aspect of getting the excitement back in your life. When you love a big goal, you become excited about waking up every morning because it is another opportunity to work towards it.

There are risks in going for a lofty goal or dream. But taking a gamble is necessary for growth. Risks lead to having an adventurous life. They are unavoidable because even if it feels *too risky* to stop what you have always been doing, chances are you will be left with never having lived a whole life.

A goal that is so big and deeply important to you brings back the skip in your step. You are striving for something, and your deep desire is so strong that it will do what it takes to make it happen.

Steve Bow said that God, the universe or life force, the magnificent, the energy that has created you, has given you more abilities than you could ever use in one lifetime. But the most significant part of you is genius. It is non-visible. It is an active part of you.

Let's repeat that. **You** possess more talent and ability than you could ever use in one lifetime. Think about that. The potential inside of you is infinite. This means that you have not even scratched the surface of your potential.

Your infinite inner genius is so powerful. It takes a big beautiful goal for you to tap into it and express it. You know the reason we have goals and plans, and you should have personal targets set to stretch, grow and make you tap into more of that infinite genius inside you so you can experience more of the truth of who you are.

You see, we don't necessarily have goals to get things, have more money, have more success, and whatever, although things make life great. But every goal you achieve allows you to experience a part of yourself that you have never had the opportunity to. That part of you has been hidden dormant deep inside you. It has always been there. It is the genuine you, but it has never been stretched enough to experience it.

You know, you're relieved because the money is there. The clients are there. Great, so that's how life should be. So, are you dancing with life, or are you struggling? Are you stuck? Because if you are, it's time to get unstuck. You were born to dance.

As Napoleon Hill said, "Success is the progressive realization of a worthy ideal."

As Napoleon Hill said, "Success is the progressive realization of a worthy ideal."

Success is great. We both love what we do. It blesses us every day. But the thing we did not expect in achieving our big goals was the most significant gift. In all of that were the jewels, blessings, and precious gems. They shine so brightly inside when you stretch yourself. It is exhilarating to pursue something so exciting that you never knew it could ever happen for you. You see, you have gems inside that are way more expensive than the most precious jewels around.

In 2015, Suzana was in Tiffany & Co.® on 5th Avenue, in New York. She had a memorable getaway with a group of girlfriends. During their visit to Tiffany & Co.®, they had a spectacular piece in a glass box. The necklace was covered in yellow diamonds. Suzana couldn't tell you how much it cost, but it was in a secure glass box with a security guard next to it, which showed it would have been worth millions. It was a really precious and stunning piece of jewelry, probably the most incredible that Suzana and her girlfriends had ever seen in their entire life.

They discovered that the remarkable Audrey Hepburn had worn it in the movie *Breakfast at Tiffany's.* The joy of admiring it was immense. They could just imagine how special she felt wearing it.

A few years after Suzana's little adventure in New York, she took a significant risk in life to pursue a childhood dream—a burning desire to have her own company. It was a considerable jump since she had never been in business before. Although it was a rough start and took a while for momentum to develop, she started to stretch, grow, and really go for her big goals and dreams. Dreams that she thought she could never achieve but started to realize with ease and flow. Each time these dreams began to fall into place, she discovered more significant and more beautiful aspects of herself than she had ever before.

She would often reminisce on those yellow diamonds - so perfect, pristine, and stunning. Yet the more she realized success and giant quantum leaps in achieving her dreams, the more evident the reward was not what she had thought. She imagined it would be the money, or the status of being one of the top consultants in the world, the wardrobe or the car would be the reward. Yes, they are lovely to have and have enriched Suzana's life, no doubt. But the biggest prize was one that she had not expected—and that was the person she had grown into. It was an internal experience. Suzana realized that her precious gems were within. She had jewels so unique that even that Tiffany & Co.® necklace with exquisite diamond was nothing compared to the gemstones and diamonds inside. No one could buy the gems within because they could not be purchased. They were priceless. So they lay dormant for years, patiently waiting for you to develop the courage to go for your big, beautiful and wild dreams, your life's purpose. And when you dare to do it, it comes together. She risked it all, and it was worth it. It is the price paid to awaken the real you and the magnificent power within.

Your goal has to be so big and beautiful to be worthy of your precious life. You are priceless. You cannot be bought. And when you stretch and grow and have your big goals, you tap into your inner diamonds, which connect to your inner jewels. We promise you that nothing compares to any challenge you have had along the way. It is nothing compared to the experience of opening up to your power and coming home to your authentic, beautiful, powerful self.

We promise you one thing when you start to stretch and grow because you decided to think big, even though your past may not have been great, it doesn't matter. Even though you're not feeling great about yourself right now, it doesn't matter. You were born for greatness. In fact, you are greatness.

That exquisite piece of jewelry was beautiful, and it's great to have beautiful things. Of course, we can wear it in all our glory, but we must never forget what it symbolizes and that our beauty is not in the jewels we wear, but it is within us. Wouldn't it be fun having something like that around your neck?

What you have lying dormant inside is way, way more exquisite. When you open up to your divinity, power and humanity, all at the same time, warmth comes through. You're attractive. You are in love and awe of yourself and your life. You're both human and divine.

So, guess what? We have goals, and that deep desire within because we don't see how we will achieve what scares us. Remember this: no matter what you've experienced, you were meant to have that goal. The reason is, that it is your gift and is intended to be yours. Your goal is your highest self calling you to dance and open up. Let go of your limiting beliefs, worries and things that keep you in a prison of limits.

So we have sizable goals and dreams and the audacity to attain them. Yes, achieving those goals is fun. It makes life fulfilling and gives it purpose. What you experience when you stretch, grow and move into more of your infinite potential is much more.

Most people only tap into approximately ten percent of their potential. A big goal stretches you to tap into more of your enormous potential. One of our favorite quotes from the great Bob Proctor states:

"The only limits in our life are those we impose on ourselves." -Bob Proctor

"The only limits in our life are those we impose on ourselves."
-Bob Proctor

Most times, we're standing in our way. Our limited belief in what we can do and what's possible has prevented us from achieving the things we want to achieve. School has taught us S.M.A.R.T. goals.

SMART Goals Acronym

- S – Specific

- M – Measurable

- A – Achievable

- R – Relevant

- T – Time stamped

If there's anything that we've learned from Bob Proctor, S.M.A.R.T. goals will limit you because you're putting a ceiling on what you're pursuing. However, once you decide on your main goal, you can then use S.M.A.R.T. goals to assist in completing the tasks on your journey.

So let's get into setting lofty goals. We've broken them down into three types. They're called ABC goals.

A TYPE GOALS - DOING SOMETHING YOU ALREADY KNOW HOW TO DO.

B TYPE GOALS - WHAT YOU THINK YOU CAN DO.

C TYPE GOALS - YOUR WANTS. WHAT YOU REALLY WANT.

An "A" goal is doing something you already know how to do. These types of goals are considered linear goals. They're not going to stretch you at all. So an example of a linear goal for myself would be if I'm going to publish a book. That is not a goal that is stretching me. I have published four books of my own. I've published many books for my clients, and I've also helped Suzana. So publishing books is not a significant goal for me.

Do you presently have goals?

Are they written down?

If you presently have an "A" goal, something that you already know how to do, write it down on a piece of paper under the heading "A GOAL."

After "A" goals, the linear goals that don't stretch you, there are "B" goals. "B" goals are doing something you think that you can do. There's no inspiration in a "B" goal. They're circumstantial goals, so there's a minimal stretch in a "B" goal. For example, a "B" goal says that if certain things were to happen, I would be able to attain this goal. It's not a goal that's far out of reach. It's giving you minimal stretch.

After "B" goals, we come to the "C" goals. The goals where your gems lie. Your "C" goals are your fantasies. They're the things that you really want to do. If you told someone in your family about your "C" goals, they'd probably think you're crazy. They are the goals you fantasize about doing. They're enormous, and you're emotionally tied to them. They are the things you truly desire but have no idea how you will attain them in this lifetime. The mere thought of your "C" goal terrifies you when you consider pursuing it.

Type "C" goals come from your fantasies. They originate through the effective use of your imagination. Think of a dream that you presently had.

What is a "C" goal that you have floating around in your thoughts?

What would be a fantasy for you? Maybe if you shared it with your kids and loved ones, they would say, "Be realistic."

Be still, use your imagination, and tap into your creativity. Everybody has creativity within them. The word creative comes from the root creator, which is within. We're created in God's image. So how are we expressing our creativity?

There's no growth in "A" goals. There's no inspiration in "B" goals. So it's about setting those "C" goals.

Think about how your present goals line up. Are they A's, B's or C's?

You were created by the highest force of creation— energy, God, the universe. So what that means about you is that you are the highest form of design. You were created in God's image, in the universal image, which is creative. Think about nature. It is abundant. When a tree bears fruit, there are hundreds of fruits on one tree, not just one piece of fruit. And that is just during one season. The lifetime of a tree bears thousands of fruits. The seeds of those fruits, when planted and nurtured, create thousands of fruit trees that bear thousands of fruits.

Lookout at the stars at night, we cannot count all of them in the sky, and we cannot see the infinite number of galaxies in our universe. Nature is abundant. And we, being a part of nature, are born to be plentiful. The same intelligence that created all of the stars, galaxies, and universes is the same intelligence and creative force that lies within you.

This energy is a creative force. It is the most powerful creative force that exists. Therefore you are nothing less than the highest form of creation that exists, and you were created so that you can continue the creative process.

So we have significant Type "C" goals to stretch and grow us. Type "C" goals help us tap into our dormant infinite power. We have no purpose if we don't have a Type "C" goal. We have stopped the creative process, and therefore, we lose the joy and excitement in life—we quickly become bored.

If you think about society today we have family dysfunction, mental health, substance abuse and an array of entrenched problems that people are experiencing. Many people are less than satisfied with their jobs, yet they hold on to their posts to pay the mortgage. They give up their lives, to live in a big house that keeps them stuck in a job they don't enjoy. Do you ever get that feeling where you dread waking up in the morning because you have to go to work?

"Boredom is your imagination calling to you." Sherry Turkle

"Boredom is your imagination calling to you." Sherry Turkle

As stated, this is why we need the big Type "C" goal because we are creative. If we're not creating, we are disintegrating. There's no inspiration if we're not expanding, growing, and using more of ourselves. What is not growing is dying.

So a Type "C" goal is something you don't know how you're going to achieve because you've never done it before. It is the goal you feel deeply excited, yet also nervous about achieving. It makes you feel this way because you do not know how to achieve it.

The Creative Process

The creative process is a term used by Proctor Gallagher Institute (PGI) to describe the journey one goes through when they have decided to go for their big goal or fantasy. Diagram 2 (taken from PGI's Thinking Into Results Participant's Guide) below shows a pictorial depiction of this journey and how a big dream or fantasy may not be possible for you to turn into a reality when you decide to go for it.

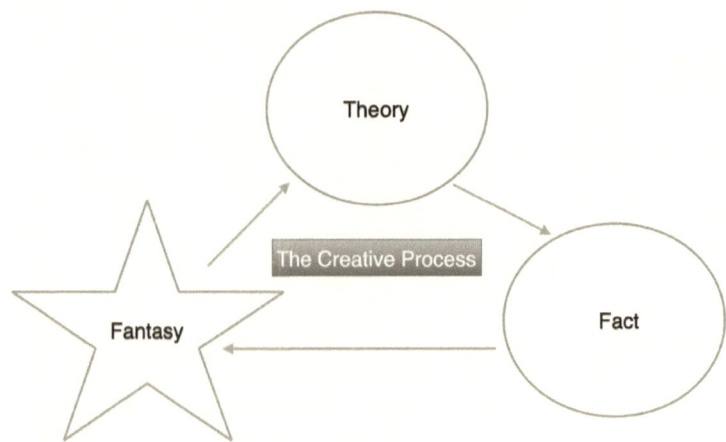

Diagram 2. The Creative Process from Proctor Gallagher Institute's Thinking Into Results Participant's Guide

Before the creative process diagram below can commence, there are two essential questions that one needs to ask themselves. The first question is:

"Am I able?"

Am I able to achieve this vital thing that scares me and makes me excited at the same time?

Am I able?

If you have infinite potential inside you if your potential and genius go on forever, are you able? Absolutely!

Yes, you are able. And, you know what? Not only are you able, but that sizable dream, the big goal that you have? It is tiny. Even though it looks big. It's small compared to what you can achieve. Know that you're definitely able. So that leads us to the next question.

"Am I willing?"

Nobody but you can answer this question. Are you willing to do what it takes?

We know that you're able because you have infinite potential. Even if you don't believe it right now, you absolutely do. But are you willing? That's only a question that you can answer. Am I willing to do what it takes? Am I willing to go through the challenges? Am I courageous enough to say yes to invest in myself, time and money so I can grow and develop?

Am I willing to go through my hero's journey? Am I inclined to not worry when people say I can't do it? I will keep going, moving towards my goal no matter what.

The Hero's Journey is Joseph Campbell's interpretation based on common themes and experiences depicted in mythology and history that a person generally goes through when they are on a journey to realizing a significant goal. Along this hero's journey, one experienced many challenges and hardships, villains and teachers, but they always won if they continued without giving up despite the circumstance. Therefore, your hero's journey will sometimes take you through a swamp. Sometimes there'll be swamp creatures—people that may not be overly positive or want you to have your dream realized. It will take you through great times as well as challenges.

Am I willing to keep going regardless of these challenges? Because the hero is the one who keeps going.

If you have answered YES to both of these questions, then the creative process begins.

So you have answered the two critical questions:

Am I able?

"Yes, I am."

Am I willing?

"Yes, I am."

Let's have a look at what happens during the creative process. Diagram 2 above shows you a visual representation of this journey.

The star represents your Type "C" goal. (refer to diagram)

Type "C" goals should be a fantasy. The way I tap into my heart is that I have a candle with me at all times. I have meditation music,

I relax, and I allow the inspiration of the music to go through me. I start to fantasize and decide. My next goal is influenced by the thing that inspires me and makes my heart sing the most. Even though it's scary, and sometimes I don't even believe that I will achieve it.

Now, as soon as you've developed the fantasy, that's one step. Many people have big dreams and never realized them. The reason why is because they are wishful—simply dreaming. We have learned that the universe doesn't conspire to help the person with the dream.

Suzana believed that the universe would conspire to help a person with a dream when in actuality it conspires to help the person who's made a decision. An actual decision means that it is done. Once the decision is made, you immediately move into action. So once you've decided to achieve your fantasy, you start moving, you naturally begin to take action.

You're on a different vibration. You start to attract different types of people, and once that happens, the universe begins to move to help and meet you with your dream. What you want is wanting you. As soon as that happens, your fantasy or dream becomes a theory.

It's a theory. It's a possibility. It's possible. It's no longer impossible, and it becomes a fact when you keep moving towards it. So you have incredible faculties inside you. You have the faculty of imagination. You have to create it. The creative process does not happen out there. It happens inside you.

The creative process is not without. You have the power to move energy through your thoughts, actions, and emotions into the creative process. Then when it becomes a fact, it's time for another Type "C" goal because once you achieve it, it becomes a reality, and it is now a Type "B" goal.

We are going to give you an assignment. I want you to get your pen and paper out.

We want you to think about what you would love.

What would you love to be?

What would you love to do?

What would you love to have, even if it feels like for any reason it's beyond your reach right now?

Give yourself time to be still. Allow yourself to relax and use your imagination.

Let your mind be free. Allow yourself to fantasize and then create a shopping list of all of the things that you want. You're going to create two lists. One for your personal wants and and another for your professional desires because these will sync. As you are fantasizing? Do not give any mental energy to how you will accomplish this goal. Do not concern yourself with where the money, time, and assistance you may require will come from—attempting to think of the "how" will either limit or destroy the fantasy.

Just think of WHAT you want.

After you've created the list, **select one you want more than anything** from each list.

You must choose something special, something you feel drawn to and is important to you. You must want it—you must really want it, with your heart and soul. It is also crucial that the wants you choose are in harmony. They must not pull you in opposite directions.

You must pick a want that connects with you emotionally—something you've always wanted and passionate about.

The subconscious mind is your feeling mind, and it is powerful. It controls a lot of what you do. So your choice needs to be something that's connected to your feelings. Write about these wants existing in your life in the present tense. Then see yourself in possession of whatever it is you want.

(Describe your wants in detail and in the present tense.)

We want you to visualize yourself in possession of that thing you want.

What does that look like for you?

What does that feel like for you?

We want you to describe it in as much detail as possible and write it out in the present tense. Then ask yourself, am I able, and am I willing?

Those are two fundamental questions. Sometimes we have these goals, haven't asked ourselves these questions, and then these goals become interests. It now becomes something that we're interested in doing that never actually gets done. We've now started to make excuses for why we can't do it instead of being committed to making that thing happen because we're willing and able. They end up on our interest list rather than the goals we desire to accomplish.

Now write your personal and professional goals on a goal card (a business card size that will fit in your pocket). You should be able to articulate your goal in one concise sentence. Look at your goal card every morning, as often as you can throughout the day, and every night. It will keep the goal at the forefront of your mind. This exercise keeps the goal connected to your will, and the drive to go after it. The constant reminder of the vision contributes to manifesting it quicker.

You have tremendous creative potential. Everything you see around you was once an idea conceived in the imagination. All images that originate in the imagination are referred to as fantasies.

Flying airplanes were fantasy at one time. So were the automobile and the internet. You begin by building a fantasy to exercise your creative faculty (your imagination). Next, you mentally start to play with that fantasy until you begin to take it seriously. Then you flip from using your imagination to using your reasoning factor, another one of your intellectual faculties, and you start to build the idea more clearly. At this point, the image turns into a theory in your conscious mind.

Before the theory can become a goal, you must ask yourself two questions.

The first question is:

"Am I able to do this?"

When you consider the only two sources of reference we have to go to concerning human potential, science and theology, both indicate that our potential is infinite. Therefore, the answer to the first question must be an emphatic YES.

The second question is quite different. It is:

"Am I willing to do whatever is required to cause the image in my mind to manifest in physical form in my life?"

When your answer to that question is yes, your theory immediately becomes a goal. When you turn your goal over to the universal subconscious mind, the laws of the universe kick in and the first law-perpetual transmutation of energy takes over. Your plan begins to move into physical form, with and through you. It causes your behavior to change and, at the same time, begins to attract to you all those things required to manifest your image. Before long, your theory becomes fact.

The three stages of creation:

1. Fantasy

2. Theory

3. Fact

This is how everything has been accomplished.

Chapter 6:

Habits

"We are what we repeatedly do. Excellence, then, is not an act, but a habit." – Aristotle

Habits are routines and behaviors that we perform automatically. They allow us to carry out vital activities such as brushing our teeth, taking a shower, getting dressed for our career of choice, and following the same routes every day without thinking about them. In addition, our unconscious habits free up resources for our brains to carry out other more complex tasks like solving problems or deciding what to make for dinner.

The best way to change your bad habits is to directly replace them with new ones. When you create a pattern, your brain makes new neurological pathways allowing you to use those habits more.

We will be covering habits and talk about how patterns work and can change your practices. But before we get started with digging into habits, Suzana will lead a meditation to help you go beyond the conscious mind and enter the subconscious mind to change self-destructive habits, beliefs, and other unconscious states of being.

When we're going for big goals or changing habits, it's imperative that we slow our thinking minds down. The limits and the boundaries keep you in prison. We connect to our energetic selves and our spirits. Let's do a short meditation.

Guided Meditation

Get yourself in a position where you're completely relaxed. Make sure you're as comfortable as you possibly can be in your chair, that your back is wholly supported and your body feels entirely supported.

Let's close our eyes.

Take a few deep breaths, and we're breathing in love and peace.

We're letting go of everything else. We're letting go of anything that's not serving us and breathing in love or your truth. Now, hold it. And when you let God let everything out, let go of your day.

Let go of your worries.

And one more deep breath breathing in, breathing in all the love of the universe here for you. Everything that you want is wanting you to breathe it in and hold.

And….let it all go.

Take your awareness to your beautiful feet. Feel the surface beneath.

Notice what it feels like.

Your feet, your beautiful feet, have carried you. They've carried you your entire life. They've brought you through the thick and thins of life. They've taken you through the dancing, running and walking— your beautiful feet. Relax the bottoms of your feet, both of your feet: your right and left foot. Completely relax your toes on your right foot and your left foot. Completely relaxed. Relax the tops of your feet, your ankles, your shins, your calves, your knees. Completely,

completely relaxed. You are relaxing your thighs all the way to your buttocks, relaxing your pelvic area.

Relax the lower part of your back, the middle part of your back and your shoulders. Completely relax. Your stomach, your solar plexus, your chest completely settled and feel the relaxation as it moves into your arms, elbows, forearms, wrists, and all the way to your fingertips or your hands. All the way to your fingertips on both of your hands, the top and bottom of your hands.

Feel the relaxation move into your neck, your voice box. Your voice is essential. You have a message. You have a gift. You are the gift. Relax your throat chakra. Feel the relaxation.

Moving to your jaw and your cheeks. Completely relaxed and around your nose and all-around your eyes.

Notice the intricate muscles around your eyes. Sometimes there's tension in those tiny muscles that we overlook. Relax your temples. Relax the top of your head, the side of your head and the back of your head, completely relaxed. Your whole body's now fully supported and completely relaxed. I feel the peace.

I'd like you to move your attention and become aware of the center of your chest—this is your heart center. It's not your heart; it's the center of your chest.

Feel the peace, the stillness, the wisdom, infinite love in the center of your beautiful chest.

Imagine a beautiful pink dusty light moving into the center of your chest, with a complete sense of letting go, a full understanding of relaxation and staying present in your center.

Bring your beautiful, big Type "C" goal to your attention. Your dream. Feel it in the space of the center of your chest. Then be with it and enjoy.

You are the gift and you have a gift. You are the gift to life, and life is the gift to you.

Notice how you feel now that your goal has been realized. Feel as though it is here right now. You have achieved it. Congratulations.

Feel how you feel in your body. How do you walk? How do you talk? How do you talk to yourself?

What is life like now that your dream has been realized?

Stay with your dream in the center of your chest. Feel the silence of that peace because your vision can become a reality. It is here for you. It wants you, and it is meant to be for you. So let's spend a moment in complete silence and stillness and notice how you feel. That might come through from the center of your chest.

What is to be yours will be yours. Relax, no expectations. Enjoy staying aware and focusing on the center of your chest, just for a minute.

Notice if anything comes up. Notice the silence. Notice the power of you.

And now, feel your beautiful goal in the center of your chest, your heart-centred. Feel the love knowing that you are love. You are infinite love. You are peace. You are intelligent. You are endless intelligence.

You are here today. You are here to love yourself and love life. Life is serving you, and without you, the entire universe would be out of alignment if you did not exist. So stay with your beautiful dream in your heart center.

Enjoy it. This is you. Feel it.

Feel the stillness, the silence.

This was meant to be yours.

Now, open up to the feeling of gratitude. Feel the appreciation from your heart. The gratitude that you exist, the gratitude of your dream, of your goal. The gratitude for being here with us today.

Thank you. Thank you. Thank you. And when you're ready, open your eyes and come back to the room.

How habits work

Can we break the habit of being who we are?

YES, WE CAN!

If you make a reasonable effort to change your thoughts and habits, life on the outside will reflect that.

How has your brain changed at all today or even this week?

You saw the same people, watched the same shows, went to the same places.

The definition of insanity is doing the same thing and expecting a different result.

The results are in the routine! The routine is in your habits. You are the creator of the loop.

If the input remains the same, the output will always remain the same.

As long as you recreate the same mind, you recreate the same life.

How can you think, feel and act differently to produce a different result? You can do so by changing your paradigm.

Do you want to know your present paradigm? Then look at your current results.

Paradigms control virtually every move you make. When you understand how to build a new paradigm to replace the one that controls your life, you will have opened the door to receiving the results you have envisioned.

A paradigm is a multitude of habits, a mass of information programmed into your subconscious mind, genetically from the moment of conception and then environmentally after birth. This information, or the paradigm, is then expressed in behavioral patterns that produce the results you receive in life.

The paradigm is what structures a person's logic, language, mannerisms, etc., and they have been programmed into us from childhood.

As you gain a deep understanding of paradigms, it becomes evident that logic on a conscious level and paradigms on a subconscious level shape a person's perception and places them in a box beyond what they can see without the effective use of their imagination.

Unfortunately, the paradigm has such an enormous influence on overusing a person's conscious faculties. If and when they use their imagination, they will generally unconsciously use it negatively against themselves. A person will create an image in their mind where they see the conditions and circumstances as the dominant role and become subservient to them.

This puts the individual in a position that prevents them from moving forward.

Culture is a paradigm that is a group habit expressed in lifestyle. Religion is a paradigm: group thinking, group habits.

Paradigms are either positive or negative, and we express them in either positive or negative results. If a person experiences recurring adverse effects, they must understand that the cause of the problem is not the circumstances or conditions outside of them but within. It lies with their paradigm.

It is the paradigm that has attracted the conditions or circumstances that contribute to the problem, and we can change it.

A paradigm is a multitude of habits. Some of these habits are good, producing wanted results or results that you enjoy. However, some habits also form the negative aspect of the paradigm that requires changing.

We realize that your paradigm is a multitude of habits and requires considerable attention and discipline before being changed. So, the question then becomes which habit we should work on, and how do we change it?

There's a quote from Bob Proctor that I love where he says:

"One difference between successful people and all the rest is that successful people take action." -Bob Proctor

"*One difference between successful people and all the rest is that successful people take action.*"

— Bob Proctor

Creating New Habits

Develop the habit of regularly connecting with your heart center where you know that you are freaking awesome. And not that you're just awesome, but that you are complete—in the now. There's nothing wrong with you. Apart from thinking that there's something wrong with you, there is absolutely nothing missing unless you *believe* something is missing.

Yes, you do have some work to do. You can feel good from reading this book and doing the exercises. You can hold the information from this book and not do anything with it. And that's absolutely okay. But it's not going to bring you the change, and we want you to have a quantum leap. So let's talk about reprogramming and how you change.

How do you change habits? We know the paradigms in your subconscious mind dictate your results. So, your results will always be according to your paradigm.

Unless you change your paradigm, nothing's going to evolve. Now the good news is that you can change your paradigm. You absolutely can. There are two significant ways you can do that. The first way is through emotional impact. But emotional impact is usually from a negative experience, for example, trauma—people who have experienced bullying or violence as a child. We all know someone who has heard of a confident driver who has an accident, but now they're afraid to get into a car. Therefore, as adults, they're so scared to connect. They're apprehensive about talking to people and being present. That's the subconscious.

So this is what happens when there's an emotional impact. It goes straight into the subconscious and aligns itself so it can protect you. So it's not enough to show up once.

It's not enough to show up to free seminars.

As adults, we have many wins and successes and some failures and challenges. But what occurs is because our childhood experiences are often a combination of some fantastic and unfavorable things.

As adults, we tend to fixate on failures, and then we repeat those behaviors because that is what we are focused on. We do it repeatedly, without even realizing what we're doing. Today, you are based on your childhood experiences and the past five or ten years. Knowing this, as an average person, you'd probably be focusing on what hasn't worked for you. But instead, those unfortunate situations have become a part of your paradigm rather than the wins.

You have 60 to 70,000 thoughts every single day. Think about that. You may have heard this. But over 90% of those thoughts are in your subconscious. So you're not even aware of what you're thinking. Your mind is on automatic pilot. The crazy thing is that those same thoughts are most likely similar to those you had as a child because of one event, two events or whatever horrible situation you may have experienced.

So you've been repeating the same sentiments over and over as an adult. You're not even aware that those thoughts are creating your results. You're expecting to have a better or different future. So you set a new year's resolution. You're like, this year, it's going to be different.

How often have you told yourself," I'm *going to lose weight this year.*" And two, three, four, five months down the road was the same as every other year. The secret is you must change those repeated thoughts and align them with your success energy so your future can change. You can do that with emotional impact backed by repetition. As we've all experienced and are aware, paradigms are difficult to change. Suzana has been in this sector for over thirty years with a background in helping professions. She has not met anyone who has been able to change their paradigm independently. You can absolutely do it. But it is rare because your paradigms are insidious. They creep up on you. That's why you need experienced and trained people to assist you. That is why we have coaches and mentors for guidance.

I'm going to give you a strategy now to change your habits.

"Whatever we plant in our subconscious mind and nourish with repetition and emotion will one day become a reality." Earl Nightingale

"Whatever we plant in our subconscious
mind and nourish with repetition and
emotion will one day become a reality."
Earl Nightingale

1. Think of a situation where you are not getting the results you want.

2. Write a detailed description of the unchanging results you are receiving. Highlight the non-productive activities.

3. Ask yourself, if you turn all the non-productive activities into productive ones, would you get the results you want?

4. On a separate sheet of paper, write down how you would love the situation to be in the present tense. For example, "I am so happy and grateful now that…"

5. Take the negative sheets of paper with the unwanted results and the non-productive activities and shred or burn them. The action is symbolic. As you are shredding/burning the sheet of paper, mentally release them. Hold a picture of yourself actively involved in the productive activities you have selected to replace the non-productive activities.

We want you to think about your daily habits and how you want the situation to be with outcome-based patterns, even while writing out this exercise. Focus on what you want to achieve while shifting your attention to who you wish to become with identity-based practices.

There's a reason for writing out the answers.

1. Writing causes thinking.

2. Thinking creates an image.

3. The image stirs emotions.

4. The emotions cause the action.

5. The action sets up a reaction.

6. It is this action/reaction that alters the conditions and circumstances or environment in our life. We refer to that as our results.

7. There is power created with the written word.

We want to make sure that you write this down. We could ask you to do the exercise and think off the top of your head, but it will not yield the same results.

When we have a negative or positive thought, it sets off a chemical reaction within the body.

Everything we do consistently, including our habits, affects us physically, mentally, emotionally and spiritually.

For example:

- Stress (or negative thoughts) can worsen physical illness
- Fear can lead to increases in certain chemicals that prepare us through the "fight or flight" response
- Ideas start chain reactions that allow us to contract our muscles

If you want to start changing your thoughts, you need to be aware of your thoughts' triggers and the patterns of ideas that you have in response to those triggers.

So we're asking you to take this exercise seriously. First, write down in detail the situation that you're not getting and the results that you want. Then highlight your non-productive actions, and on a separate piece, write down how you would love it too. Lastly, shred the non-productive results.

Stages of Habit

In James Clears' best-selling book, *Atomic Habits: An Easy & Proven Way to Build Good Habits & Break Bad Ones*, he breaks down a framework for getting 1% better every day by mastering tiny behaviors that lead to remarkable results. As one of the world's leading experts on habit formation, Clears intertwines ideas from biology, psychology, and neuroscience to create a simple guide for making good habits inevitable and bad habits impossible.

All habits go through four stages in the same order.

The habit loop:

1. Cue

2. Craving

3. Response

4. Reward

The four stages of habit are best described as a feedback loop. They form an endless cycle that is running every moment you are alive. This habit loop continually scans the environment, predicts what will happen next, tries out different responses, and learns from the results. The cue triggers a craving, which motivates a response, provides a reward, satisfies the craving, and ultimately becomes associated with the cue.

In the beginning, a habit requires a good deal of effort and concentration to perform. It gets easier after a few repetitions but still requires some conscious attention. With enough practice, the habit becomes more automatic than conscious. Beyond this threshold—the habit line— you can do the behavior more or less without thinking. A new routine is being formed.

There are three layers of behavior change:

3 layers of behavior change:

1. Outcome

2. Processes

3. Identity

With outcome-based habits, the focus is on what you want to achieve. With identity-based habits, the focus is on who you wish to become.

The difference between a good day and a bad day is often a few productive and healthy choices made at decisive moments. These choices stack up throughout the day and ultimately lead to very different outcomes. Each one is like a fork in the road.

The process of mastery requires that you progressively layer improvements on one another, each habit-building upon the last until a new level of performance has been attained and a higher range of skills has been internalized.

Chapter 7:

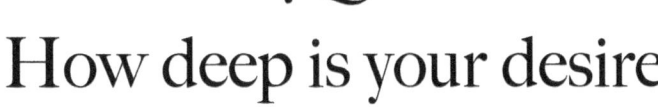

How deep is your desire

"Human behavior flows from three main sources: desire, emotion, and knowledge." - Plato

The depth of your desire for change will determine whether the modification you are seeking will be permanent. Arguably, the greatest philosopher of our time, Neville Goddard, stated, *"All transformation begins with an intense, burning desire to be transformed."* Therefore, change must come through you first and foremost. You must want to renew your mind and for the change to take place. The deeper your desire for a profound effect, the more assured the change will occur.

One of our most significant paradigms is that circumstances or situations outside ourselves are primarily the reasons for our states, livelihoods, and experiences. It is an illusion we are taught to believe. We have not been schooled to take responsibility for our results in our society. However, accepting responsibility for every part of your life will get true freedom.

According to Goddard, the truth is your 'state of consciousness is the cause of your results, experiences and what you do or do not have in your life. You must be the person you want to be, and you must have the thing you want in your awareness first. Then you must completely renew your mind. Meaning, that you must completely let go of who you thought you were, what you thought you could have, and wholly become the person you want to be. First, you must be aware and then entirely immerse yourself in being or having that thing before it can manifest. This is what it means to renew your mind. Then finally, you completely abandon the old way of being and fully and wholly become the new person.

It is similar to Einstein's saying, "Insanity is doing the same thing over and over and expecting different results." We must change our minds first and merge in the consciousness of what we want. Re-birthing or recreating yourself and your life are necessary to see the changes and manifestations come into play.

A person who chooses to stay in bitterness, resentment, and anger for past failed relationships can never attract an excellent relation-ship. The change must happen on the inside initially before they can manifest a beautiful, fulfilling relationship. But the desire must be strong enough for the individual to want to change. Furthermore, they must be substantial enough to abandon old ways because sub-conscious paradigms can be challenging to change, as we have al-ready covered in this book.

When the desire is strong enough, renewing your mind (the change in your self-image and paradigms) no longer has to be a struggle. The desire itself becomes more substantial than the paradigm or the fear.

The thing that you want the most is also wanting you. It is ready to manifest. But it cannot do so without it coming through you first and foremost. Your mind is the center of divine operation. This means that manifesting anything - whether it be your soulmate, a successful business, money, or a new home must come through you. The desire must be strong enough so that when you merge with it completely, it must be so without a flicker of doubt. You direct the energy, and it needs to work through you. Become one with it through your mind, body, and entire way of being.

You must become it. You can do it by using one of the most potent faculties in your mind—your imagination. Imagine things are the way that you would love them to be. Then, use your imagination to create an image. Once you have it in mind, connect with that emotion—and then live from that state, think from that state, experience from that state— BE that state.

You are here to create and expand your consciousness of who you indeed are. You being here in your physical state is evidence that you are great. You have greatness inside you. Manifest that deep desire in your heart. It is meant to be yours. Align with it wholeheartedly, and it will align with you. When the time is right, it will manifest in the physical.

That is why permanent transformation begins and ends with renewing your mind.

We hope this book has inspired you and you walk away with a renewed mind. Maybe you are thinking about giving yourself some grace and living in the moment. Perhaps you imagine all of the dreams you can now take action on to become a reality. But on the other hand, you could be thinking about all of the non-productive habits you are prepared to replace with new routines.

Things will go wrong. You may lose patience with a loved one, or worse, with yourself. Maybe a necessary appointment may be canceled, or you may break a glass or wake up late for work. When you wake up tomorrow morning, your paradigm will kick in, and you will start to doubt, worry or fear taking action.

Reading a book, listening to a podcast or attending a class isn't suddenly going to make everything in your life perfect. Circumstances will never be ideal, and perfection is not the goal. Instead, life is full of beautiful imperfections for us to appreciate along the way. Understanding this will help prepare us for whatever comes our way.

We have to honor the present moment and be grateful for its lessons. If we don't learn the lesson, it will show up until we do. So, pay attention to how you feel, process and choose your desired vibration (feeling). God has a plan for our life, but we were given the ability to select and make decisions along that path. We have the power of choice.

You can choose fear, or you can choose faith. Choose wisely. They are both beliefs in the unknown. Faith believes in your desired outcome. It feels that things are working out for our good. No matter the circumstance, things are working out for our good. Faith believes that God collaborates with you to make your dreams come true. Lastly, faith believes that your Type "C" goals will manifest because you have everything inside of you that you need to make anything happen.

"For as the body without the spirit is dead, so faith without works is dead also." James 2:26

"For as the body without the spirit is dead, so faith without works is dead also." James 2:26

We can transform our minds to believe in our potential, but we must also take action. As you do so, appreciate the process. Be grateful for who you are becoming.

Understand that embracing ALL of you, loving yourself and your perfectly imperfect bits, is part of tapping into your full potential. The more we appreciate ourselves, the more we are likely to stick to habits and routines that are good for us and replace those that are not. So let this journey of breaking through your fears and forming productive habits be more profound than simply achieving material goals. Let it be a journey of building a deeper connection with your higher self.

Let this be the beginning of RENEWING YOUR MIND.

Moving Forward

"Baby steps count, too, as long as you're moving forward." -Chris Gardner

Renewing Your Mind Community

If you've enjoyed this book and would like to explore further how you can tap into the truth of who you are and feel supported, join the Renewing Your Mind Community.

Renewing Your Mind is an online mindfulness and personal development community. We guide thousands of women from all around the world in transforming their life by renewing their minds.

Join Makini and Suzana Live each week to dig deeper into awareness and consciousness. Every month we go live with structured masterclasses where we share strategies, resources and frameworks to help you uncover your hidden potential based on years of study and firsthand experience as mindset coaches.

As a member, you will get access to recorded sessions, live sessions and a community of like-minded women on their journey of transforming their inner and outer world. We unpack thought-provoking books. We ask questions to help you open up and remove blockages. We cover topics from mindfulness, well-being, career, spirituality and more.

For more information, please go to

Facebook.com/RenewingYourMind

About The Authors

~

Suzana Mihajlovic

"Suzana is one of my top people in the world." - Bob Proctor

Suzana Mihajlovic, elite-level performance and mindset coach, has had a wide calibre of experience and expertise, distinguishing her from the ordinary. She has been referred to as the "missing link between success and failure."

Suzana is one of the few Proctor Gallagher Institute Consultants who worked very closely with Bob Proctor himself. She is one of his best. She is in his Inner Circle and is one of the very few who have received a Pin directly from Bob in his Circle of Excellence. Receiving a pin from Bob Proctor means that the great man himself has acknowledged that you are top in your field.

Suzana has applied the principles that she teaches to her own life and has, during this time, expanded her client base to all over the world. Her international success coaching company, Your2Minds, has clients from every continent (except Antarctica). She is also a best-selling author.

Suzana has always held a passion for human greatness. She has had a gift for seeing one's potential and how an individual can overcome barriers/challenges to achieve much higher levels of success in their chosen area.

Suzana has many Degrees, Diplomas and Certificates from various Universities. These include a Bachelor of Arts (Psychology) from Deakin University and Post Graduate studies in Health Counselling and Business. She has also studied at Ashridge University, United Kingdom and was one of a small number of international students who completed studies at Hiroshima City University, Japan. Before founding Your2Minds, she held several senior management positions in the helping professions.

Suzana is a highly sought professional in mindset and human potential. She has led major public speaking events and shared the stage with the world's most outstanding leader in human potential, Bob Proctor himself.

About The Authors

Makini Smith

"Makini has a personal magnetism
that draws people to her."
- Linda Proctor.

Makini is an award-winning entrepreneur and proud founder of A Walk in My Stilettos. As a mindset coach, she has created a successful business focused on personal development and helping women thrive. She is also a certified Proctor Gallagher consultant, a podcast host, a 4-time author, and a social media influencer. She has had the honor of being mentored directly by the late Bob Proctor, his wife Linda Proctor and his daughter Colleen Proctor.

She's the founder of Legacy Leavers Media, helping women entrepreneurs self-publish with the same tools and resources as traditional publishers without the need for their validation or approval.

She has been nominated for the Peoples Choice Award for Best Black Canadian Podcaster as host of the 5-star rated 'A Walk in My Stilettos' podcast. One of the top 1.5% most popular podcasts globally, it focuses on inspiring women to conquer their fears, own their stories, and strengthen their resilience.

Makini's goal is to help women improve their quality of life while spreading awareness about the importance of mindset. She has shared her expertise on global media platforms, including Chatelaine, xoNecole, iHeart Radio, CBC, Vice News, a Times Square billboard, and more. Makini is a 5-time nominee for the RBC Women Entrepreneur Awards. In the 2018 Canadian Election, she ran for Provincial Parliament to enact positive change and lead by example.

Makini helps her clients turn dreams into reality, shift their mindsets, and become best-selling authors leaving a legacy.

www.ingramcontent.com/pod-product-compliance
Lightning Source LLC
Chambersburg PA
CBHW031416120626
46545CB00006B/2146

* 9 7 8 1 9 9 9 0 2 4 0 4 8 *